The One-Minute
Temper Tantrum
Solution

Ronald Mah

The One-Minute
Temper Tantrum
Solution

Strategies for Responding to
Children's Challenging Behaviors

CORWIN PRESS
A SAGE Company
Thousand Oaks, CA 91320

For information:

Corwin Press
A SAGE Company
2455 Teller Road
Thousand Oaks, California 91320
www.corwinpress.com

SAGE Ltd.
1 Oliver's Yard
55 City Road
London EC1Y 1SP
United Kingdom

SAGE India Pvt. Ltd.
B 1/I 1 Mohan Cooperative
    Industrial Area
Mathura Road, New Delhi 110 044
India

SAGE Asia-Pacific Pte. Ltd.
33 Pekin Street #02-01
Far East Square
Singapore 048763

Printed in the United States of America.

Library of Congress Cataloging-in-Publication Data

Mah, Ronald.
The one-minute temper tantrum solution: strategies for responding to children's challenging behaviors / Ronald Mah.
    p. cm.
Includes bibliographical references and index.
ISBN 978-1-4129-5720-5 (cloth: acid-free paper)
ISBN 978-1-4129-5721-2 (pbk.: acid-free paper)
    1. Temper tantrums in children. 2. Anger in children. 3. Attitude change in children. 4. Child rearing. I. Title.

BF723.A4M34 2008
370.15'28—dc22   2008003607

This book is printed on acid-free paper.

08   09   10   11   12   10   9   8   7   6   5   4   3   2   1

Acquisitions Editor:	Stacy Wagner
Managing Editor:	Jessica Allan
Editorial Assistant:	Joanna Coelho
Production Editor:	Cassandra Margaret Seibel
Copy Editor:	Youn-Joo Park
Typesetter:	C&M Digitals (P) Ltd.
Proofreader:	Anne Rogers
Indexer:	Jean Casalegno
Cover Designer:	Lisa Miller
Graphic Designer:	Lisa Riley

Contents

Acknowledgments   **vii**

About the Author   **ix**

Introduction   **1**

1. Orderly Assessment to Successful Intervention:
   Where Do You Start? Where Do You End Up?   9

2. Developmental Factors: Developmental Energy Will Reassert   17

3. Situational, Physical, and Disruption Factors: 2 + 1 = Trouble!   29

4. Temperamental Factors: They Were Born That Way!   39

5. Systemic Factors: The Savior   49

6. Specific or Specialized Factors and Moral Factors: Try Harder   59

7. Four Types of Temper Tantrums! Not Always About
   Power and Control   71

8. Manipulative Tantrums: Power and Control   81

9. Upset Temper Tantrums: Distress   91

10. Helpless Temper Tantrums: Not Distress but Despair   101

11. Stress and the Cathartic Tantrum: Releasing the
    Cathartic Tantrums   111

12. Getting It Wrong and Getting It Right   119

Conclusion   **131**

References   **135**

Index   **141**

Acknowledgments

I sat in the cardboard box in the backyard, sullenly upset and trying to punish Mom and Pop with my suffering. Do they see me? Are they already missing me? There had been some parental edict that had come down against me. It's kinda cold out here. Brrrrr! But the temper tantrum wasn't working! The silent treatment, a form of temper tantrum, doesn't work so well when they don't notice me doing it!

This book is dedicated to my mother and father, Lana and Fred Mah, who raised the five of us to be good kids, good sons and daughters, good students, and, eventually, good citizens. They came from China to gain opportunity for themselves and their children, all of whom were born here in the United States. Although they disciplined from their Chinese roots, they also somehow empowered and supported us to be successful Americans. Five children . . . five college graduates . . . five professionals . . . and twelve grandchildren—nine currently college students or college graduates, with three sure to follow educationally in their time. I'm sure we acted out . . . a little, threw tantrums . . . a few! Sometimes no-nonsense and sometimes sensitive and nurturing, they gave us expectations, boundaries, and nurturing, while empowering us. Despite cross-cultural challenges, they allowed us our personal journeys and processes. Pop passed a few years ago. Mom still takes care of two of my nephews regularly after school.

Thanks, Mom and Pop, for being too sharp to be tricked by my shenanigans (I think that's an old Chinese term for "mischief!"). Thanks for helping me become the person, educator, therapist, and citizen I have become. And the clients, students, and others I've been privileged to influence owe you gratitude as well, for your wisdom and care is often passed on.

PUBLISHER'S ACKNOWLEDGMENTS

Corwin Press gratefully acknowledges the following peer reviewers for their editorial insight and guidance:

Linda Eisinger
2005 Missouri State Teacher of the Year
Teacher Grades 3 and 4
Jefferson City, MO

Elizabeth Engley
Professor of Early Childhood Education
Department of Curriculum and Instruction
Jacksonville State University
Jacksonville, AL

About the Author

**Ronald Mah,** an educator and licensed marriage and family therapist, has worked in early childhood education for 16 years, during which he has owned and operated a child development center. He is the author of *Difficult Behavior in Early Childhood* (Corwin Press, 2006) and wrote the Asian Pacific Islander Parent Education Support curriculum (DHS-San Francisco, 1996). Ronald has also worked as a trainer and has been a speaker in several DVD presentations on child development and behavior (Fixed Earth Films) and has been involved in community and high school mental health clinics, severe emotional disturbance school programs, vocational programs for at risk youth, welfare-to-work programs, and Head Start. A former community college and current graduate college instructor and member of the board of directors of the California Kindergarten Association, Ronald combines concepts, principles, and philosophy with practical techniques and guidelines for effective and productive results. Ronald is on the Ethics Committee of the California Association of Marriage and Family Therapists and has his own practice in San Leandro, California.

Introduction

FOUR TYPES, FOUR UNDERLYING ISSUES, AND FOUR APPROACHES = THE ONE-MINUTE TEMPER TANTRUM SOLUTION

1. "Ahhhhhhh!" (flaying on the floor) "Ahhhhhhh!" (peek to see who's looking) "AHHHHHHH!" (hitting a higher pitch). "I'm going to hold my breath, if you don't let me have it! Give it! Give it!"

2. "Ahhhhhhh! Nooooo! No! (sniff) No! No! (sniff) No! I don't like it!! (sniff) Please! Please! Please . . . ! I don't want to! PLEASE! Waaaah!"

3. "Ahhhhhhh! I was here first! She pushed me! That's not fair! She always gets to go first! I never get to go first! NO! . . . NO . . . No! . . . No . . . no! . . . no . . . It's . . . not . . . fair . . ."

4. "Ahhhhhhh! (deep breath) Yeah, yeah . . . (sniff, sniff) What? . . . (deep breath, deep breath) . . . I'm OK now."

Isn't there just one simple magical solution to all the tantrums? To put it succinctly, "No!" This or that self-appointed expert (who, me?) will present the magic plan or perfect prescription on how to raise the perfect child or student, with or without sound experience, research, or logical theories. Some adults look for another magical teaching or parenting plan rather than examine who and how they are as teachers or parents. Something "new" sometimes works like magic. Normally, the "magic" comes from clarity of logic. There is no real magic or magical techniques, but when you are conceptually clear regarding the reasons behind behaviors, it is almost magical how readily you can make appropriate teaching or parenting decisions.

This book presents a conceptual foundation that can keep tantrums from becoming your horror story. Each of the four tantrums described above have distinctly different qualities. If you cannot tell the difference among these four types of temper tantrums, you and your child could be in for a lot of frustration, because there are four matching interventions or approaches for handling each type of tantrum. Many children can be challenging, and tantrums are, perhaps, the most challenging behavior. Standard techniques for support, intervention, and discipline often work wonderfully well. Other times, these standard techniques are not quite wonderful but rather unmitigated disasters! There is something distinctive about the behavior or the tantrum; otherwise, the "regular" responses do not quite address the child's underlying energy. When the adult response should work, what is going on that it doesn't work? The principles to support all children are basically the same: nurturing, boundaries, and guidance. Children's response to support or lack of effective support is basically the same: depression, anxiety, frustration, accrued stress, low self-esteem, and acting-out behaviors. Temper tantrums and other dysfunctional and disruptive behavior may erupt and become habitual. Unaddressed or ineffectively handled (FOUR types of temper tantrums? Oh my!), longer-term social and emotional damages can lead to future relational, academic, and vocational failures. Ominous folk tales and professional warnings often terrify caring adults rather than empower them to effectively discipline children.

> Children's response to support or lack of effective support is basically the same: depression, anxiety, frustration, accrued stress, low self-esteem, and acting-out behaviors.

> Externalizing behaviours such as temper tantrums and management difficulties (e.g., non-compliance) were associated with adult convictions, in particular with violent offences . . . studies have shown an association between temper tantrums at age 8–10 years and a range of difficulties in adult life in both genders, including downward social mobility and divorce . . . the association between temper tantrums at age 3 years and adult violent crime is maintained when these other factors are controlled for. (Stevenson & Goodman, 2001, 192–202)

More than a temper tantrum, but budding juvenile delinquency and candidacy for the FBI's 10 Most Wanted List! Less apocalyptic, but still worrisome is Dr. Wegmann's (2007) recommendation:

> Children older than 4 who have such tantrums should be evaluated by a professional . . . Temper tantrums in children between the ages of 1 and 4 are normal. Tantrums that go beyond this age, especially if they are frequent, severe, and associated with aggressive behavior,

are a sign of a larger behavioral problem. These children are at risk for having more serious behavioral problems later in life. Children older than 4 who have such tantrums should be evaluated by a professional.

Although seeking professional consultation may be prudent for some children, adults would be well served to evaluate their own tantrum. This book will help with this.

MEETING THE CHALLENGE AND SUPPORTING CHILDREN

Age of child and the percentage of children who throw temper tantrums:

18 to 24 months: 87 percent

30 to 36 months: 91 percent

42 to 48 months: 59 percent

On average, tantrums lasted for

- two minutes in one-year-olds
- four minutes in two- to three-year-olds
- five minutes in four-year-olds

and occurred

- eight times a week for one-year-olds
- nine times a week for two-year-olds
- six times a week for three-year-olds
- five times a week for four-year-olds (Potegal & Davidson, 2003)

You always wanted the children you care for to be special! You have children who tantrum way longer and way more often than average. Lucky you. You would be ecstatic if your children's tantrums only lasted a few minutes! If you have a 5-year or older child in your class who still throws tantrums, statistics do not offer you any comfort. Many older children, teenagers, and other adults throw temper tantrums as well. For some, the problem is the frequency, whereas for others, it is the violent intensity or disruption; for others, it's the whole package. Temper tantrums truly challenge adults, and children need appropriate support when they tantrum. That support, however, needs to adjust to meet the specific underlying issue (potentially, four different underlying issues) of the particular tantrum. Handling the tantrum well has profound consequences in many areas of a child's overall development, over and above relieving the adult of the negative behavior (the screaming, stomping, swearing, or throwing!). The book will emphasize the relationship of various emotional, social, psychological, and other developmental theories in the socialization process of discipline. In addition, to benefit from and apply the knowledge of this book, one must understand the different styles by which various people and children throw temper tantrums. Not all tantrums involve throwing oneself crying and screaming red-faced on the floor. A tantrum could be throwing a fit, throwing a toy, throwing down a huge piece of chocolate cake, or, as individuals get older, throwing down a six-pack of beer, throwing a charge card on the counter, throwing away relationships, or throwing caution to the wind. As definitions of acting out and temper tantrums are merged, the applicability of the concepts broadens into many areas of childhood and adult lives.

> A tantrum could be throwing a fit, throwing a toy, throwing down a huge piece of chocolate cake; or as individuals get older, throwing down a six-pack of beer, throwing a charge card on the counter, throwing away relationships, or throwing caution to the wind.

PREVENTION STARTS WITH KNOWLEDGE AND RECOGNITION: EIGHT CONCERNS

A list of steps from Down Under, on the Australian Parenting Web site for dealing with persistent or severe tantrums (Raising Children Network, 2006), is representative of many approaches available. This list includes common recommendations and some suggestions that prove problematic upon closer examination.

1. Keep a diary of your child's tantrums for 7–10 days. Record the day . . . where it happened, what happened just before it, and what happened right afterward.

The first step may be useful for some teachers and parents in applying the other steps, or more formal than necessary for others. The next three steps are the most helpful.

2. Identify the situations that make tantrums more likely to occur. Plan ways of avoiding those situations or making them less stressful for your child.

3. Identify the triggers for your child's tantrums. Look for ways of reducing or avoiding tantrum triggers.

4. Identify the consequences of the tantrum. Can you see ways that the behavior is being accidentally rewarded by your actions or the actions of others?

This book examines and expands extensively on Steps 2, 3, and 4, using different terminology. The next steps have the potential to be useful but also to be problematic or ineffective.

5. Establish a reward system to give your child extra encouragement for staying calm.

6. Help your older child learn and practice coping skills in situations where he or she would normally have a tantrum.

Step 5 may be useful if all it takes is rewards or encouragement. That becomes nearly impossible for a child in full tantrum. Offering a reward when the child is in tantrum mode may inadvertently reward the tantrum (depending on what type of tantrum it is). For other types of tantrums, it would have negligible effect and potentially intensify the tantrum. Practically speaking, a calm child is the default setting, normally neither noticed nor rewarded. Step 6 is essentially socialization. Socialization is usually completely forgotten in the full arousal of the tantrum for both the child and the adult. The eruption of tantrum for toddlers and older children means that socialization has been overwhelmed. Many experts very unfortunately echo the last step and recommendations of the list.

7. Here are two possible options when your child throws a tantrum:
   • Ignore the tantrum: do not look at or speak to your child while they tantrum.
   • Use time-out.

Ignoring a tantrum may be the worst thing to do when a child throws a tantrum. Ignoring a child flies against the fundamental premises of child development. The recommendation comes from an often false assumption of the child's motivation to tantrum. This book explains the logic and the underlying illogic of ignoring a tantrum (besides that, it usually doesn't work!). Time-out as a strategy is based on a false belief that avoiding punishment effectively overwhelms any underlying motivation. Furthermore, it is based on the simplistic but inaccurate assumption that all tantrums are about power and control. For a detailed discussion on the three problematic theories and the one effective theory of time-out, you may want to read my book, *Difficult Behavior in Early Childhood: Positive Discipline for PreK–3 Classrooms and Beyond* (Mah, 2007).

In this book, readers will learn how to assess eight potential factors or issues that challenge children and how these may ignite temper tantrums. The eight areas of concern are presented in a progressive sequence for assessment. Although some issues are commonsensical, others are more complex and potentially problematic. There is significant discussion of developmental principles, temperamental traits, systemic influences on children, and particularly challenging conditions that create greater vulnerability to frustration, acting out, and temper tantrums. Adults can keep intervention simple through progressing through these issues. Simpler theories or issues should be examined first, and more complex ones considered after earlier interventions prove insufficient. Successful application of this hierarchal investigative process prevents the very harmful assumptions of the eighth set of issues.

> Readers will learn how to assess eight potential factors or issues that challenge children and how these may ignite temper tantrums.

Failure to recognize what you are dealing with or incorrect assumptions about what is happening is likely to frustrate the child and make things worse for the both of you. What's worse than a child throwing a tantrum? A child and an adult both throwing tantrums back and forth! "Remain calm and do not argue with the child. Before you manage the child, you must manage your own behavior. Spanking or yelling at the child will make the tantrum worse. Think before you act. Count to 10 and then think about the source of the child's frustration . . ." (Harrington, 2004). "1, 2, 3, 4 . . . I'm thinking about MY frustration!" Aggravation caused by the child's tantrum ignites us all too often. When we are frustrated, we are not calm, do not think, and become argumentative! In addition to the four approaches for addressing the four underlying issues of the four tantrum types, the book presents a fifth intervention approach for dealing with a tantrum when you cannot quickly identify the type of tantrum. This allows for recovery after initial adult frustration and failure with handling the tantrum. It finally all comes together in the "One-Minute Temper Tantrum Solution," in dealing with an active tantrum.

THE ONE-MINUTE TEMPER TANTRUM SOLUTION

I can hear the screaming and crying from my office (I'm the director of this preschool). It has been going on for a couple of minutes. I can hear Mickey screaming, "It's my turn!!" and the teacher screaming, "No, it's not! You can't run this group! You stop it!!"

Here they come again! The teacher stomps into my office, with Mickey in tow. Angrily, she puts him on the couch, "He's got to learn he can't just have his way all the time! I don't have time to deal with his tantrums!!" She stomps off to rejoin her group of three-year-old kids, which is now, of course, in chaos.

Tears are streaming down Mickey's face; his face is red; his entire body shakes with the hiccups. I turn my chair toward him. . . . Less than a minute later, he has calmed down, acknowledged how he needs to behave, and goes off to rejoin his group where he is able to cooperate again. Why? What had been going on? What happened? What did I do?

When someone throws a temper tantrum, whether he or she is an adult, teen, child, colleague, or supervisor or employee, we often get sucked into a miserable, fruitless, and escalating battle. Who was throwing a tantrum? Mickey was, but so was the teacher! She couldn't handle him, when he desperately needed to be supported. Even as she began the battle, she already knew that it was going to be fruitless and escalating. We get into stupid arguments with children and adults. You realize that you are saying the same thing over and over again . . . and so are they! There seems to be no gracious way to end the argument without losing something precious— perhaps our self-esteem? When we are finally done, we chide ourselves for having fallen into it again! Later, we think what a stupid argument it all was. Yet we get emotional, physical, fight to the death, divorce, or even risk our livelihood or employment. We berate and humiliate children, and we berate ourselves in our own frustration and humiliation.

What was so important to fight for so vehemently and to risk so much? It could not have been just whether the child dropped or threw the toy . . . whether you already told the child and he or she had heard you clearly. Or whether the other employee took five minutes longer at lunch. The facts of the situation are almost irrelevant compared to the underlying issues of the tantrum or argument. What appears to the outside objective observer as a nonsensical argument or tantrum over trivial matters is, to the participants, a desperate life-and-death struggle to maintain their sense of worth, self-esteem, and rights. Many teachers and parents discipline from the frustration of their own life experiences, acting out personal, emotional, and psychological turmoil with children. The information and guidance presented in this book has to pass through your personal process before you interact with a child. Instincts and intuition are often good guides to discipline, but personal work is necessary to tell the differences between instincts and intuition and your neuroses! Each of the four types of tantrum has high potential to ignite adult reactivity that exacerbate or interfere with resolving the tantrum. Personal resolution and development creates healthy adults who are best suited to support children. Such adults are able to give and receive respect and affection. Their core values and identities to be conscientious individuals and community members are reflected back as children internalize the modeled morals. Healthy adults recognize others' power and control issues from their own healthy sense of power and control. They also create secure boundaries in the home and classroom where children can flourish without fear of rejection or abandonment. The intensity of temper tantrums often ignites fundamental issues and raw nerves in adults that waylay positive responses. Children need adults to provide positive responses from the very beginning. It starts with a teacher welcoming his or her class on the first day of school. For parents, it starts in infancy. Children have the greatest need for healthy and wise adult responses at the times of their greatest needs. They often express that greatest need with behavior that we call temper tantrums.

> Each of the four types of tantrum has high potential to ignite adult reactivity that exacerbate or interfere with resolving the tantrum.

You thought that I was going to give you the One-Minute Temper Tantrum Solution in the introduction? Nope! Now, don't have a hissy fit! Get your tea or coffee or glass of wine (or Red Bull), get comfy in your favorite chair, take a deep breath, and turn the page. As you read, you'll find there will be many One-Minute Temper Tantrum Solutions, whether they actually take a minute, a couple of minutes, or more. I was able to handle Mickey's temper tantrum in less than a minute. Most important, no matter how long it may actually take, once you gain the background and understanding, you can more efficiently and effectively handle all the tantrums and acting out thrown at you.

CHAPTER HIGHLIGHTS

- There are four different types of temper tantrums with four different underlying issues that require four different interventions.
- Meeting the challenge and supporting a child's temper tantrum facilitates self-esteem, social skills, and psychological health, increasing options and future success; failure, on the other hand, can lead to many future problems.
- Prevention starts with knowledge and recognition of eight potential tantrum triggers.
- Misunderstanding tantrums results in adult responses that cause greater problems for children and adults.
- Personal resolution and development create healthy adults who are best suited to support children, even when they are throwing a tantrum.

Orderly Assessment **1** to Successful Intervention

Where Do You Start?
Where Do You End Up?

Oh my gosh! I can't believe she could do that! You wouldn't think something that big could fit into something that small! Okay . . . it's discipline time. Time to do the old discipline thing . . . or is it, the new discipline thing?

Where do I start? How do I start? Reason with her? Distract? Do expectations? Trick? Motivate? Coerce? Punish? Threaten?

Wait . . . what's the tantrum all about anyway? A maturity thing? Circumstances? Fatigue? Hunger? Getting sick? A disruption? Personality? Are we all nuts? Is there something wrong or off? Did the devil make her do it?

It's not just discipline time! It's the daily discipline detective time!

IN LOVE WITH YOUR HAMMER

What happens when you fall in love with your hammer? Everything starts looking like a nail! Bam! Bam! Bam! Many people discipline with one technique or from one perspective only. The perspective may differ among adults, but they have in common the assumption that there is only one reason for the behavior or misbehavior. Therefore, only one approach or discipline is necessary. A significant percentage of parents of preschoolers use corporal punishment to discipline their children, despite the spankings not working to eliminate the behavior! Straus and Stewart (1999) report that the use of corporal punishment reaches its peak at 94 percent at the ages of 3 and 4 years. Straus (1994) interviewed 270 individuals regarding their experience of the year they received corporal punishment the most, which was around age eight. Barely half felt that the corporal punishment was effective. In addition, spanking became less effective as they grew older. Forty-two percent reported hating their parents for the spanking. Rather than arguing whether spanking is appropriate and/or can be effective discipline, of concern are parents who continue to spank despite it clearly not being effective. Such parents may have stuck with spanking because this may have been their original model from their childhood and there had been little reexamination of more appropriate or more effective discipline. Someone will ask me, "Is it OK if I _____ my child?" My normal response is, "Does it work?" A common response is, "Well . . . not really." Then I throw up my hands in mock exasperation and ask, "Then why are you asking me if it's OK!?" Dakota tribal wisdom says, "When you discover that you are riding a dead horse, the best strategy is to dismount and get a different horse." Not only are people stuck in applying discipline that does not work, they seek permission to continue riding that dead horse! "Is it okay if I ignore my tantruming child, even though she gets even more distraught?" "Is it okay if I hug the tantruming child, even though he pushes me away and continues screaming?" "Is it OK to spank if it doesn't work with my child?" No! It isn't OK! On another level, when individuals claim that a technique works, the next examination needs to be on the accompanying costs and effects. Straus and Stewart (1999) are among researchers who find many major harmful effects from using corporal punishment. Discipline techniques are tools to deal with behavioral issues. As with all tools, they can be properly or improperly applied to a task. A tool may not be effective for the task or may work for

> A parent or teacher must judiciously choose the appropriate approach, tool, or intervention to address the discipline or behavioral issue at hand.

the task while damaging it. You can use a hammer to drive a screw into wood, but both the screw and the wood will be damaged. A tool chest contains many different tools. One does not randomly reach into the toolbox and grab just any tool. A parent or teacher must judiciously choose the appropriate approach, tool, or intervention to address the discipline or behavioral issue at hand. Children are far more precious than screws. Don't screw up!

ASSESSMENT, NOT ASSUMPTIONS

Distinguish common behavioral issues with more complex or more severe and less common challenges. If problems persist, professional consultation is highly recommended, as opposed to hoping that children will "grow out of it." Be sure to find the right professional. Although many parents turn to their children's pediatricians, their expertise is primarily in medical health and physical development. Early childhood educators, teachers and other educators, developmental specialists, neurologists, speech and language professionals, mental health professionals, vocational therapists, and other specialists are often more appropriate to consult depending on your child's issues. Various individuals focus understanding children's temper tantrums by identifying situations or triggers. Janet Lawrence (2007), whose expertise includes experience raising a child with autism, gives a list of situations when the child may throw a temper tantrum. Some of the situations are self-evident and relevant to nonautistic children, whereas others may be unique to her or a child with autism:

1. Getting dressed for school

2. The kitchen guessing game

3. The car ride—the child safety seat, going backward

4. The car trip through town

5. Public places

6. Helium balloons

7. Potty training

8. The doctor's office

9. A one-track mind

10. Perfectionism

School psychologist Robert Harrington (2004) writes,

[T]here are predictable situations that can be expected to trigger temper tantrums, such as bedtime, suppertime, getting up, getting dressed, bath time, watching TV, parent talking on the phone, visitors at the house, family visiting another house, car rides, public places, family activities involving siblings, interactions with peers, and playtime. Other settings include transitions between activities, on the school bus, getting ready to work, interactions with other children, directives from the teacher, group activities, answering questions in class, individual seat work, and the playground. (p. 1)

The Web site MamasHealth.com (2007) offers a list of "What Triggers a Temper Tantrum?":

- . . . [being] inadequate in their abilities to master a new toy or activity
- not [being] allowed to wear clothing they prefer, or eat and drink what they want
- overstimulation
- being confined in a car seat or stroller for a long period of time
- denial of a request
- being separated from something or someone they love
- a change in their routine

Although there is validity in naming situations and triggers, there are no comprehensive lists, nor are they necessarily applicable to the tantrums of other children, teenagers, and adults. Similar and dissimilar issues or a combination of issues might trigger the different tantrums listed. A "magic wand" solution is not available, and smacking all tantrums with a hammer approach is dangerous. These and other triggers and situations, however, can be conceptualized into categories or theories of factors that guide prevention and intervention of temper tantrums. The following hierarchy of factors or theories can help one understand a particular child's behavior and may also be considered areas of potential issues that ignite temper tantrums.

AN ORDERLY APPROACH FOR UNDERSTANDING BEHAVIOR

1 year old, 3 years old, 6 years old, 10 years old, 13 years old, 17 years old. . . 44 years old!?

1. Development ⟶ **2. Situation**
Two kids and one toy! ⟶ **3. Physical condition**
Sick, tired, or hungry?

4. Disruption ⟶ **5. Temperament**
happy happy **happy**
angry angry **angry**
sad sad **sad** ⟶ **6. Systemic**

7. Specific conditions ⟶ **8. Moral**

This hierarchy was developed for parents, teachers, and social services professionals who requested a systematic process to understand the motivations behind child and adult behavior. Children may exhibit the same behavior for any of several different reasons or from some combination of reasons. For example, a child may act out due to fatigue, poor modeling, impulsiveness, frustration, and so forth. Although it is usually necessary to set boundaries regarding a behavior, adults also need to understand the factors that cause the behavior in the first place. Punishment may stop the child's immediate behavior, but the behavior may repeat. Underlying issues that continue to exist may erupt into tantrums. Each of these eight sets of factors, issues, or theories may be considered areas in which poor response by adults can ignite a temper tantrum.

> Children may exhibit the same behavior for any of several different reasons or from some combination of reasons.

The orderly assessment or diagnostic process starts from a developmental perspective to progressively higher levels of concern. For many children, several issues may apply. Some people have a favorite theory to explain why children behave and, as a result, always look to that theory for guidance. Although some people love a particular technique (e.g., the hammer), other people love a particular perspective (e.g., hammering) that explains everything for them. In *The Great Santini,* a movie (Carlino, 1979) based on a novel by Pat Conroy (1976), Robert Duval plays a Marine Corps fighter pilot who believes in military discipline not only in his military life but also in his family life. When he applies this concept to relationships with his wife and children, they suffer great pain, disconnection, and disruption. One teacher may discipline children from the perspective of setting boundaries and punishing negative behavior. That teacher assumes that once the child is punished for violating a boundary, the behavior will stop. Another teacher may think that the child is acting out to attract nurturing attention. That teacher gives big hugs, with the expectation that the need for nurturing will be satisfied and the negative behavior eliminated. These responses may be intervention without assessment and may prove ineffective. They do not consider other possible relevant issues (e.g., the child has high energy, may be distractible, is a six-year-old who has started kindergarten a year late, may be tired, plays a lot of violent video games, has emotionally neglectful parents, is in a poorly managed and crowded classroom, may be frustrated because of a learning disability, and is overexcited because it's almost Christmas). Both teachers could have missed possible relevant theories about hyperactivity, attention deficit, development, fatigue, social modeling, family dynamics, environmental influences, learning disabilities, or sensory thresholds relevant to this child's behavior. Teachers may continue unsuccessful interventions with a whole slew of negative consequences. One underlying theory may be more convenient, but it is neither appropriate nor effective if it's a dead horse. Pull out the entire tool chest! There is no single tool or magic wand that will "presto-chango" solve all the problems.

PLURALITAS NON EST PONENDA SINE NECCESITATE

Some parents or teachers cherry-pick the issues that they feel they can handle and ignore the ones that are challenging or uncomfortable. For example, if unfamiliar with recognizing and handling learning disabilities, they may ignore helping the child to compensate for the disabilities. Teachers may be defensive about their classroom structure and excessive levels of noise and activity. If uncomfortable with confronting family dysfunction that affects children's behavior, they work in isolation from the home influences. The teacher can easily become more and more frustrated. The child will feel negativity from the teacher and also be frustrated from failing in the classroom. The child may act out and or throw temper tantrums. Each of these issues and other factors become potential tantrum igniters when handled poorly by adults. The first four sets of issues are very commonsensical but sometimes forgotten when adults are under stress. Some adults have a tendency to make things more complicated than necessary.

> *'Pluralitas non est ponenda sine neccesitate'* or 'plurality should not be posited without necessity.' The words are those of the medieval English philosopher and Franciscan monk William of Occam (ca. 1285–1349). . . . What is known as Occam's razor was a common principle in medieval philosophy and was not originated by William, but because of his frequent usage of the principle, his name became linked to it. (Carroll, 2006, ¶ 1–2)

A more modern and blunt version would be the K.I.S.S. principle— Keep It Simple, don't be Stupid! Sometimes, teachers or parents scare themselves with more complex and convoluted theories about behavior, when very often, a simpler perspective may be adequate. If you have a headache, for example, it may be prudent to drink a glass of water because of possible dehydration rather than scheduling surgery for a brain tumor! Keep It Simple—you can be Successful. Keep It Simple, don't Scare yourself! The following are the eight factors or issues:

1. Developmental factors (including life-cycle issues for adults)

2. Situational factors (other children, colleagues, availability of toys and/or resources)

3. Physical factors

4. Disruptional factors (from specific circumstance)

5. Temperamental factors

6. Systemic factors (environmental or ecological)

7. Specific or specialized factors

8. Moral factors

The first two sets of issues (a total of six), when forgotten, cause people to move too quickly and dangerously into the last two issues. The last two issues or theories can, if applied too quickly, cause problems for everyone. If parents or teachers understand the behavior's cause as normal or expected, there is a high tolerance for the behavior and general acceptance. If they do not recognize or accept the issue or factor as relevant, the tolerance can be much lower and the judgment highly negative. I present more extensively about the factors and issues underneath behavior or the igniters of temper tantrums. Clarifying how important these issues are to children significantly aids dealing with tantrums in the present and the long term. Adults get away with inefficient and conceptually unsound methods of handling the tantrums of babies and very young children. However as children get older, the sloppiness of the adult tantrum response is exposed, and adults eventually run into enraged adolescents who were failed as toddlers and younger children when they tantrumed. Dr. Les Parrott (2000) writes,

> the anger of adolescents is like a buoyant basketball forced under water: hard to sit on. When the delicate balance required to hold it down is disturbed, adolescent anger comes rushing to the surface and explodes into the environment. In children we call it a temper tantrum, but the same experience can be seen in many adolescents. When a fit of anger is provoked in adolescents, the reaction may be almost volcanic in intensity. . . . While tantrums are expected in young children (ages two to four years), destructive rage is out of bounds for adolescents. Often adolescents who throw tantrums have benefited from them by watching their parents raise the white flag of surrender in the face of angry fits. (p. 83)

> If parents or teachers understand the behavior's cause as normal or expected, there is a high tolerance for the behavior and general acceptance.

Anger from being ignored, dismissed, and frustrated is held down by adult intimidation and young children's lack of mobility and resources.

Adolescent mobility and access to other (including peer) resources breaks the balance. Teen behavior can become explosive, when adults can no longer get away with inefficient and now ineffective discipline. This comment on toddler behavior is actually a warning: "Some call this stage the terrible twos and others call it first adolescence because the struggle for independence is similar to what is seen during adolescence" (Harrington, 2004, p. 2). Catching tantrums and handling them successfully when children are younger become critical in avoiding the retreat and surrender adults face as children become older and bigger—as they eventually become teenagers struggling for independence and the out-of-control adults who do not value interdependence in the community. Tantrums occur and must be dealt with during the first adolescence of toddlers and the regular adolescence. They occur and must be handled in relationships in the extended adolescence of the twenties and the double teens . . . and at ages forty-sixteen and seventy-eighteen! They may occur in different sizes and in various guises, but they will erupt. Temper tantrums are part of life and relationships, but we don't have to surrender to their potential destructive forces.

> Catching tantrums and handling them successfully when children are younger become critical in avoiding the retreat and surrender adults face as children become older and bigger—as they eventually become teenagers struggling for independence and the out-of-control adults who do not value interdependence in the community.

CHAPTER HIGHLIGHTS

- Many people persist with one discipline technique from one perspective or theory for understanding behavior, whether or not it works.

- Tantrum triggers and situations can be put into categories or theories of factors for an orderly assessment process that guides prevention and intervention.

- Adults can scare themselves with more complex and convoluted theories about behavior, rather than starting with more simple interpretations that may be effective.

- Developmental factors, situational factors, physical condition, emotional condition, temperamental factors, environmental and ecological factors, pathology, and morality are eight perspectives for assessing children's behavior.

- Adults can get away with inappropriate discipline for younger children in their "first adolescence" struggle for independence, but eventually, enraged adolescents expose the ineffectiveness with explosive behavior.

Developmental Factors

2

Developmental Energy Will Reassert

Water . . . water . . . gotta find water. Wonderful smooth water. Feels so neat. Goes through my fingers . . . in my mouth . . . everywhere. Water . . . where's the water? Go wash up for snack? Wash my hands with . . . water! Oooooo! Cool water . . . warm water . . . splish splash . . . water in the sink . . . on the walls . . . splish splash . . . water on the floor . . . Oooooo!

Stop it!? But . . . Oh, all right . . .

Snack time . . . Crackers, a piece of apple, and juice . . . juice? Juice! Looks like water . . . with color and pulp . . . and a different taste! Oooooo! It goes through my fingers . . . splish splash . . . on my face . . . everywhere . . . splish splash. Oooooo!

Stop it!? Mess? Oh, all right . . .

Go out to play? Okay. Oooooo! It rained last night! Puddles! Oooooo! Splish splash! Splish splash with my hands! Splish splash with my feet! Oooooo! With mud! Oooooo! . . . my shoes . . . on the fence . . . on Jenny! . . . on Greg!

Stop it!? Why? Mess? But . . . Oh, all right . . .

Almost time for lunch? Time to go potty? Okay. Go to the bathroom . . . with the sink and . . . the toilet!! Oooooo!! Oooooo!! YES!!

1. DEVELOPMENTAL FACTORS AFFECTING TANTRUMS

Is what the child doing okay for children of his or her age? Although behavior may be challenging (or messy or loud), it also may be age-appropriate behavior. Being fidgety, throwing tantrums, putting things in the mouth, touching everything, can't stop making noises is . . . fine for a six-month-old! That's OK. And for a one-year-old. Still OK. And for a four-year-old. A bit of concern. And for a 35-year-old! Uh-oh! Greater concern derives from expecting individuals to internalize socialization about sitting still, touching things, and being quiet, and for self-regulating behavior. When developmental energies and expectations are misunderstood, greater problems arise from failure to satiate them in safe and appropriate contexts. Many challenging children are developmentally young. Three sets of problems may arise from development issues. Younger children may not have made sufficient progress to communicate their needs, thus becoming frustrated and being more likely to throw a tantrum. Second, younger children often still have strong motor-kinesthetic tendencies from sensory motor development. American classroom teaching is often visually oriented and may mismatch the learning style of the child. As more time is dedicated to skills development for testing in elementary schools, there is less free play, exploration time, and outside playground time. Being unable to meet high energy and touching motor-kinesthetic needs in a strongly visual or auditory-oriented program can make behaving difficult for the child. If motor-kinesthetic needs are satisfied, the child is better able to attend, sit quietly, not touch, and so forth. Third, children who have suffered from excessive stress, abuse, or trauma tend to regress or get stuck at more immature developmental stages.

> When developmental energies and expectations are misunderstood, greater problems arise from failure to satiate them in safe and appropriate contexts.

Many adults tend to focus on management issues, which may ignore needs the child is trying to fulfill. Satisfying these needs is essential to a child's emotional or psychological balance; social, cognitive, and physical maturation; and holistic development. The principle of developmentally appropriate practices is key to facilitating the growth of children through various stages. In each stage, there are particular needs and issues, abilities and limitations, and challenges and tasks to address. The movement from one stage to another depends on a combination of experiences, learning, and maturation. Within each stage, growth is primarily incremental or a matter of quantity. Quantitative growth is small increases of strength, greater frequency, better ability, and more of this or that. Babies and children gradually increase abilities in many areas. Eventually, new qualitatively distinctive stages of development arise, and babies can do new and wonderful things that are fundamentally different. This occurs in intellectual, physical, social, and other areas of development. The National Association for the Education of Young Children (2007) reminds educators and parents the following:

> Domains of children's development—physical, social, emotional, and cognitive—are closely related. Development in one domain influences and is influenced by development in other domains. Development in one domain can limit or facilitate development in others. . . .

Developmentally appropriate practices require supporting and challenging children in ways that are appropriate to their developmental stages in all areas. If adults are unclear where their children are developmentally in any area, they may inadvertently frustrate developmental energy by pressuring children beyond their developmental capacities. Children will feel incompetent and lose self-esteem as they struggle and fail at tasks beyond their developmental competency.

> In each stage, there are particular needs and issues, abilities and limitations, and challenges and tasks to address.

JUST PLAYING

The classroom is alive with enthusiastic energy. Some children are painting with thick tempera paint. Several are intensely engaged with the dress-up clothes. Four children are passionately negotiating the castle layout and the story line around the Legos— ". . . and then, the dragon flies into . . . " Three children repeatedly pour sand into large bowls in the sand tray. Other children are making their own books. Four children are in the loft reading to each other. Johnny has joined Sue with the puzzle they took out. It's PERFECT! As the teacher, you're managing the energy and flow, but it's easy—the children are so involved! Suddenly, your serenity is shattered as an observer (parent, administrator, reporter) says, "When are you going to teach something? The children are JUST playing."

A career kindergarten teacher told how her inner-city students, many with significant socioeconomic burdens, desperately needed time to play. With tremendous pressure to raise test scores, more classroom time was dedicated to developing skills for testing. As outdoor and free play was reduced, children were more stressed, acted out, and had more social and relational problems, including tantrums. They lacked time to practice social emotional development and communication skills. Children in every stage of development have unique needs and challenges from developmental energy that will continually assert until satisfied. The resistance of children to do more formalized instruction (typical of standards-driven curriculum) and their continual drive to play indicates that play is the primary developmental task of that stage. National Association for the Education of Young Children (2007) says

> Play is an important vehicle for children's social, emotional, and cognitive development, as well as a reflection of their development. Understanding that children are active constructors of knowledge and that development and learning are the result of interactive processes, early childhood teachers recognize that children's play is a highly supportive context for these developing processes. . . . Play gives children opportunities to understand the world, interact with others in social ways, express and control emotions, and develop their symbolic capabilities. Children's play gives adults insights into children's development and opportunities to support the development of new strategies . . . play leads development, with written language growing out of oral language through the vehicle of symbolic play that promotes the development of symbolic representation abilities. Play provides a context for children to practice newly acquired skills and also to function on the edge of their developing capacities to take on new social roles, attempt novel or challenging tasks, and solve complex problems that they would not (or could not) otherwise do. . . . Research demonstrates the importance of sociodramatic play as a tool for learning curriculum content with 3- through 6-year-old children . . . play serves important functions in children's physical, emotional, and social development. . . . Children express and represent their ideas, thoughts, and feelings when engaged in symbolic play. During play a child can learn to deal with emotions, to interact with others, to resolve conflicts, and to gain a sense of competence—all in the safety that only play affords. Through play, children also can develop their imaginations and creativity. Therefore, child-initiated, teacher-supported play is an essential component of developmentally appropriate practice. . . .

Compared to the short childhood of other genera, the relatively long human childhood allows for advanced cognitive (as well as social, emotional, and psychological) sophistication of the mammalian brain. Play is what distinguishes mammalian and human childhood from other genera! For example, the play between a child and a puppy promotes both of their cognitive development. Modern technologically advanced American and Western European societies, compared to other societies in the world, allow for children to have long childhoods. Over the past century or so, American children have experienced a childhood almost doubled in length, from about 13 to 25 years. Seth Godin (2005), a marketing guru and author of several books, strongly advocates play as critical to creativity and success. As a therapist, I see couples who have difficulty being playful also having more relationship problems. An extended childhood reflects youth's need to continue experimenting and playing with the environment as they negotiate increasingly more complex technological and social worlds. If our society is to be serious about better developing our youth, then educators need to be serious about making sure that children play! And frustrating children's attempts to play causes temper tantrums!

BASIC RULES OF DEVELOPMENTAL THEORIES

All adults, not just educators, need to be aware of other principles of development besides play. Ruffin (2001) presents these principles:

1. Development proceeds from the head downward . . . the cephalocaudal principle.

2. Development proceeds from the center of the body outward . . . the principle of proximodistal development that also describes the direction of development.

3. Development depends on maturation and learning. Maturation refers to the sequential characteristic of biological growth and development.

4. Development proceeds from the simple (concrete) to the more complex. Children use their cognitive and language skills to reason and solve problems.

5. Growth and development are continuous processes.

6. Growth and development proceed from the general to the specific.

7. There are individual rates of growth and development.

Such principles of development were augmented to create the following basic rules of development and developmental theories. When adults ignore or don't understand the basic rules, they create developmental crises for children that often erupt into tantrums.

1. Development happens in **STAGES**.

2. There are **CRITICAL PERIODS** in development when the person is more vulnerable to harm or available for growth.

3. **QUANTITATIVE** changes lead to **QUALITATIVE** change. Small increases in quantity (amount, frequency, skill, etc.) lead to significant quality differences or movement into another stage.

4. Development is **SEQUENTIAL**. There is an order to development.

5. Development is **PROGRESSIVE**. Development in the earlier stages set up development in later stages.

6. **SKIPPING** or **RUSHING** development doesn't work and/or causes harm. Developmental demands that are skipped or rushed will pull the person back for completion or resolution until they are completed. You can get stuck or regress to such stages until they are resolved.

7. Excessive **STRESS**, **ABUSE**, or **TRAUMA** will get people stuck or to regress at earlier stages. Such extreme experiences draw a person's energy and attention away from dealing with or resolving the developmental needs of the stage. (Skipping or rushing development creates stress in and of itself.)

8. **DEVELOPMENTAL ENERGY** will eventually reassert itself.

9. **RESILIENCY** allows for skipped, rushed, incomplete, stalled, regressed, or suppressed development to be restimulated in the organism.

10. **SATIATION** of developmental needs allows for progression to the next developmental challenge. Until the developmental needs of the stage are met, an individual will stay in the stage.

DEVELOPMENTAL ENERGY AND SATIATION

Play can be defined, from the work of Piaget (1953), as the experimentation and exploration of the world that stimulates cognitive and other areas of development. The foundations of lifelong issues, including attachment, self-esteem, mastery, reading skills, eating habits, and so forth, are established in early childhood. In each stage, children have quantitative experiences (being able to stack two blocks, then three blocks, etc.; understanding and speaking one word, then two, then three, and so forth; learning social management vocabulary— "please," "thank you," "share," "turns") that lead over time and experience to a great leap forward into a substantially qualitatively different stage. Examples include the ability to arrange blocks to create symbolic structures; to put words together to express thoughts; or to negotiate complex social interactions. Important developmental energies and needs require resolution in each stage. These become critical periods, when children are simultaneously more highly vulnerable to negative experiences and highly receptive to extensive development. The National Association for the Education of Young Children (2007) says, "At certain points in the life span, some kinds of learning and development occur most efficiently. . . . Although delays in language development due to physical or environmental deficits can be ameliorated later on, such intervention usually requires considerable effort." For example, children find second language acquisition considerably easier in the early childhood versus later years (personal and professional observations). Many of my clients have lingering issues from developmental needs unfulfilled during critical periods. Development is also sequential and progressive. The National Association for the Education of Young Children (2007) says,

> The foundations of lifelong issues, including attachment, self-esteem, mastery, reading skills, eating habits, and so forth, are established in early childhood.

> Development occurs in a relatively orderly sequence, with later abilities, skills, and knowledge building on those already acquired. Human development research indicates that relatively stable, predictable sequences of growth and change occur in children during the first nine years of life. . . . Predictable changes occur in all domains of development—physical, emotional, social, language, and cognitive. . . .

Development is also progressive. The challenges and successes (and the failures and incomplete accomplishments) of earlier development build for (or cause problems for) future development:

> Early experiences have both cumulative and delayed effects on individual children's development; optimal periods exist for certain types of development and learning. Children's early experiences, either positive or negative, are cumulative in the sense that if an experience occurs occasionally, it may have minimal effects. If

positive or negative experiences occur frequently, however, they can have powerful, lasting, even "snowballing," effects. . . . For example, a child's social experiences with other children in the preschool years help him develop social skills and confidence that enable him to make friends in the early school years, and these experiences further enhance the child's social competence. Conversely, children who fail to develop minimal social competence and are neglected or rejected by peers are at significant risk to drop out of school, become delinquent, and experience mental health problems in adulthood. . . . Early experiences can also have delayed effects, either positive or negative, on subsequent development.

The development of secure attachment with primary caregivers creates the ability to risk and succeed at attachments within subsequent relationships. Conversely, insecure early attachment makes it difficult for children (and later as adults) to form secure attachments. The quality of the parent–child attachment predicts the intensity and degree of difficulty of separation anxiety and accompanying tantrums. Whatever is not experienced or achieved earlier in life (especially during critical periods) causes subsequent problems or potentially persistent deficits later in life. Relative to play, the long-term emotional, psychological, relational, and social problems with adults include the following:

- an inability to play with their own children;
- an inability to play (relate healthfully) with partners;
- difficulty being spontaneous or creative;
- fear of exploration and experimentation (rigid and overly conservative or cautious behavior).

Attempting to rush or skip development causes harm, problems, and tantrums—and quite simply doesn't work! Intrinsic developmental energy will continue to assert itself until the needs are met. For example, many babies have a very strong oral need. For various reasons (cultural, recommendations from family or "experts"), when parents frustrate oral satisfaction, children often continue beyond kindergarten putting things into their mouths. Limiting play and other developmental energies to achieve mandated performance standards risks creating a generation of developmentally incomplete people. Rushed or skipped development causes individuals to become increasingly stressed and frustrated. Temper tantrums and/or the battles between children and adults are often children's developmental energy trying to assert itself despite blockage by adults. Trauma, abuse, and intense stress can overwhelm the developmental process of an individual. They draw the individual's focus away from satisfying their developmental needs. Subsequently, faced with intense stress, including being frustrated or blocked, individuals may emotionally or psychologically regress to or get stuck at those earlier developmental stages where they hope to be nurtured and protected. Under stress, children may get whiny and pout, waiting for someone to feel sorry for them. "You know what Susie did to me!?" Under stress, adults get whiny and pout, waiting for someone to feel sorry for them! "You know what the boss did to me!?" Developmental energy that has been rushed, skipped, or repressed will assert itself eventually, often with pent-up, undifferentiated, self-destructive, and socially irresponsible explosions. Adolescent rebellion from suppressed developmental needs for autonomy is a classic example. The teen or adult "plays" with a desperate intensity, often creating drama and trauma for others.

> Temper tantrums and/or the battles between children and adults are often children's developmental energy trying to assert itself despite blockage by adults.

Adults may act like a two-year-old throwing a tantrum or seem like a defiant adolescent. Denying children the time and opportunity to play portends continually having to battle with their regression to meeting play needs later: in the next class, next school, in families, and in the workplace.

KEITH, GO PLAY IN THE WATER

The last two rules of developmental theories allow for hope and growth: resiliency and satiation. Critical periods are not absolute periods. Resiliency allows for developmental energy not resolved during a critical period to be addressed later, although with greater difficulty. For example, individuals who suffer major early attachment issues can experience reparative relationships with new nurturing people. The reparative relationships develop successful attachment and intimacy where none had been established previously. Satiating developmental energy is the primary intervention. As a developmental need is identified and allowed to be satiated within appropriate boundaries, an individual moves on to the next developmental challenge. Recognizing needs as developmental energy and facilitating the complete satisfaction of these needs becomes the key to helping children progress.

Keith was driving everyone crazy. He was always in the water or having an argument about playing in the water. "Keith, stop playing in the water." "Keith, get out of the water." "Keith, stop making a mess!" Keith was driving teachers to tantrums! And everyone was driving Keith crazy! The more we restricted Keith, the more maniacal he became about getting into the water. Keith threw tantrums! What was wrong with him? You would think he's sensory-motor or kinesthetic!? Duh! That was exactly what he was! Most of the other children were past that stage.

What mattered, however, was that Keith was responding to his need in his sensory-motor stage. The adults were inadvertently rushing or trying to skip his developmental process. Keith could not choose to not play with water; it was too compelling. If he could only satisfy himself, he would stop. When we figured this out, I told the teachers to stop disrespecting Keith by dismissing his developmental energy. We needed to allow for its satiation in an appropriate context. Once we realized this, it was easy.

> Resiliency allows for developmental energy not resolved during a critical period to be addressed later, although with greater difficulty.

We filled a sink with warm sudsy water (and placed mats on the floor!). For the next two weeks, every time I saw Keith, I would drop an apron on him and tell him, "Keith, go play in the water." He luxuriated in the sink full of warm sudsy water loaded with spoons, ladles, cups, bowls, funnels, and colanders. Splish, splash, splish, SPLASH! What a ball he had! Splish splash . . . splish splash . . . water was flying everywhere! Keith loved it! He tried to take a bowl of water to the house play area, but allowance for exploration and experimentation includes boundaries. "No Keith, you cannot play with water over there. Only in the sink." Keith had a ball for about 20 minutes. Then he went on to play somewhere else. The next time he passed by, again we told him to "Keith, go play in the water!" Over and over that morning, "Keith, go play in the water!" Finally, Keith stuck out his pouty lip and in a sad voice, proclaimed, "I dun' wanna to play in water no mo'! Wanna play outside . . . pleez?" By 10 a.m. each day, he would be satiated and not want to play in the water anymore. After two weeks, because his need to play with water was recognized and respected as a sensory-motor developmental need and satiation was facilitated in an appropriate context, his developmental need was met. Keith went on to his next developmental challenges. And the adults were not frustrated. Keith's and the teacher's tantrums ended. And his self-esteem remained intact. He moved onto the other developmental tasks, rather than being kept stuck by adults. He achieved performance standards as a natural consequence of healthy development. A one-minute temper tantrum solution, once we figured it out.

CHAPTER HIGHLIGHTS

- Behavior that is unacceptable at earlier ages causes concern when children are older, because of expectations that socialization would have occurred.
- When adults overfocus on management issues, inappropriate practices develop that harm the development of children through important challenges and tasks.
- Developmental energy constantly seeks to be satiated. Developmental energy will continually reassert, perhaps as a tantrum, even against adult resistance.
- Play is a critical developmental process that facilitates all areas of development, including intellectual and academic development, social-emotional development, creativity, fine-motor skills, and gross-motor skills. Without play, children become stressed and miss opportunities to practice social-emotional development and communication skills.
- Attempting to rush or skip development causes problems and temper tantrums. Trauma, abuse, and intense stress cause regression or getting stuck developmentally, which can appear as a temper tantrum.

Situational, Physical, and Disruption Factors

3

2 + 1 = Trouble!

I saw it first.
> *No you didn't! I saw it first.*

No you didn't . . . you lie! I saw it first.
> *No you didn't. I have it now.*

Give it to me. That's not fair!
> *Yes, it is fair. Because I had it first and saw it first.*

No you didn't!
> *Yes I did!*

Didn't! And, you had it yesterday.
> *So what?*

Give it to me. It's my turn.
> *No it's not!*

I'm going to tell on you!
> *You big turkey head! Ahhhhhhh!*

2. SITUATIONAL FACTORS

Two kids and one new toy truck! Five people in the family and one bathroom! A pile of bills and a pittance of income! Sounds like trouble! Sometimes, the situation—usually a shortage of resources, such as toys—is the main cause of a problem or tantrum. Changing the availability of resources, by making another toy available, for example, may be an effective approach. Socializing children to share the resources can be effective as well. For example, teach them how to take turns. Conflict and accompanying negative behavior may arise in anticipation of a shortage of resources (e.g., who will be first in line for recess or first in the line of shoppers for the early-bird after-Christmas sale). An impending tantrum may come from the child's reaction to various physical environmental circumstances. A tantrum based on not getting what a child wants should not be unexpected to the adult. If the child can alter the situation, then directing the child to do so would be appropriate. The more control a child has, the less likely he or she is likely to tantrum. Design and supply the child's individual and social environments as much as possible to create environments, so that there are/is

> Sometimes, the situation—usually a shortage of resources, such as toys—is the main cause of a problem or tantrum.

- enough toys of the same type so as not to force a level of sharing beyond the children's capacity;
- a place to go when needed for quiet time alone;
- time and room to be active and loud;
- appropriate times and support for transitions;
- toys that are developmentally appropriate; age-challenging toys, not frustrating toys;
- access to nurturing and appropriately limit-setting adults;
- access to adults who can model and facilitate appropriate social interactions;
- space, atmosphere, displays, and decorations that convey safety and security for the child.

If there are enough resources, conflict may not arise. If the child or someone else can efficiently and promptly influence the environment to meet the child's needs, the child is less likely to tantrum and more likely to stop tantruming. If other children shared previously, the child will have more confidence that other children will share again. If the child has learned a social model of sharing scarce resources, then it is less likely that he or she will tantrum. If these are true, then the One-Minute Temper Tantrum Solution is easy. OK, now let's get real. You're not reading this book to find out "if . . ." happens or works in certain situations or with certain children—rather, you need to understand what should be done when "if . . ." doesn't happen. There may be other important issues to consider that prevent common solutions from working.

The tantrum that comes from difficulty handling scarce resources or competition or adult priorities (rather than the child's priorities) becomes what many tantrum experts characterize as "demanding tantrums"

(Motamedi, 2007; Pawel, 2007; Schmitt, 2006b; Suburban Pediatric Clinic, 2007). Here is a similar description: "Manipulative tantrums" are "tantrums used to get something the child wants, like a candy bar at the grocery store" (SmartMomma.com, 2007). Other names include "Attention-Seeking or Demanding Tantrum" (Bright Horizons Family Solutions, 2007), or "Instrumental Tantrum," which is described as children's attempt "at getting something they want" (DuPree & Wells, 2007). Ignoring, distracting, indulging, punishing, or setting boundaries on these tantrums may not address the underlying issue that the situation may arouse. If there is no deeper underlying issue, then addressing the scarcity or availability of resources—"the situation"—should suffice in handling the tantrum. However, what is aroused may be what causes the tenacity of the tantrum. Several tantrum experts (including Bright Horizons Family Solutions, 2007; Motamedi, 2007; Schmitt, 2006b; Suburban Pediatric Clinic, 2007) characterize demanding tantrums as attention seeking. This differentiation or nuance offers some clues. Attention seeking may serve getting one's needs or demand met, but it also implies that the attention itself is important. This combining of demand and attention may be inaccurate and misleading. A demand is functional, such as getting a toy or candy bar, which is what can be described as the "demanding-manipulative-instrumental-attention seeking- pain in the . . . uh, tantrum." Attention or attention seeking implies an emotional or psychological need. In the later discussion differentiating manipulative tantrums and upset tantrums, this is further explored.

> Ignoring, distracting, indulging, punishing, or setting boundaries on these tantrums may not address the underlying issue that the situation may arouse.

It is often impractical to have several sets of a particular toy or multiple expensive electronic gadgets. This situation thus requires children to learn how to share resources. Community resources (bowls or buckets) of crayons or toys require that the children learn social, emotional, and communication skills and manage time to share. If the children did not share in their families, sharing may be quite a challenge for them. In addition, some children can let go of their frustration or challenges, whereas others cannot. "Certain temperamental qualities may influence a child's response to frustration. Overt displays of anger are less common in the youngster who is naturally placid, positive, and adaptable. Tantrums are more frequent in the active, determined child who has difficulty accepting limits and coping with disappointment" (Leung & Fagan, 1991, p. 559). More compliant and adaptable children respond to a resource crisis differently from more intense or inflexible children. With experience, children can learn how to self-monitor and self-regulate successfully, including negotiating the sharing of toys. However, if you leave it to them at early developmental stages, some children are likely to be disappointed and will soon express disappointment by acting out or throwing tantrums. On the other hand, if children are developmentally or otherwise able to activate the suggestions in dealing with a limited resources situation (share), then all is well. If they cannot, despite reasonable access to resources, developmentally appropriate guidance to share, negotiate, and delay gratification, then you should move forward to examine if the next set of factors are relevant. If not development . . . if not situational . . . then, maybe . . .

3. PHYSICAL FACTORS

The physical condition of the child—being sick, tired, or hungry—often affects his or her behavior. Children's mood or their sensitivity to tolerate stimulation or triggers often goes down when sick. Many teachers get a call or a note that Angel will not be coming to school today because Angel is sick. The proverbial lightbulb explodes over their heads! They now understand that Angel's behavior and illness are related, as they recall cranky acting-out behavior and bickering on the playground yesterday. Adults, in retrospect, realize that a child who is sick today was acting up yesterday! Getting children healthy is the logical approach.

Many tantrum experts note fatigue or frustration from fatigue as key in tantrums (Bright Horizons Family Solutions, 2007; Motamedi, 2007; Schmitt, 2006b; Suburban Pediatric Clinic, 2007; among others). Although fatigue can lead to frustration, frustration can also be emotionally, cognitively, and socially based. Later discussion about upset tantrums clarifies this. Physical fatigue, however, definitely turned the little sweetheart Betsi into the grumpiest little girl! Everyone was being mean to her. Nothing went the way she wanted. Sullen tantrum. Can't draw. Crying tantrum. "Johnny is looking at me! Don't look at me!" Screaming tantrum. Betsi was the only child of a single mother. Rather than jumping to the conclusion that there was inadequate parenting, remember the K.I.S.S. principle. Was it a developmental issue? No. Was it a situation where children were conspiring to make her miserable? Of course not. Was it a physical condition or factor? Hmmm? She was healthy as a horse. Tired? Betsi's mother was a community activist who, when she attended evening meetings, had to take her daughter along. Betsi would get to bed an hour or so later than normal. Extremely conscientious, Mom would bring Betsi to school at the normal early-morning time, not realizing that Betsi was more tired than usual. Subsequently, her mother warned us if her daughter was a bit short of sleep. So as soon as Betsi started to fall apart, we would put her to nap, even if it was as early as 7:15 a.m. or

7:30 a.m. A nap for Besti was for everybody's well being. "Ahhhhh! I don't want to go to sleep!" Within five minutes, she would be asleep. She would miss all morning activities and wake up after 11 a.m. She missed being miserable, grumpy, and snapping at everyone. She missed negative energy and responses that would have broken down her self-esteem. The children missed having her being nasty and grumpy (not!). The teachers missed her tantrums (not!). She woke up her normal cheery self and was able to anticipate enthusiastically for the rest of the day. A one-minute temper tantrum solution.

School free-breakfast and free-lunch programs have become a mainstay for many children. It's hard to be able to learn or otherwise function on low blood sugar levels. Mari was a second grader who was not doing well in her core topics of math and reading but did fine in music, art, P.E., and language arts. Using the orderly approach, first developmental issues and then any issues about scarce resources or the situation were considered. It turned out to be unnecessary to consider any academic issues. Mari's stressed single mother of four children fed them dinner at 5:30 p.m. and put them to bed by 6:30 p.m. Mari would not eat breakfast. As a result, 18 hours passed from the last time she ate the night before the time she would eat lunch. With nothing in her system in the morning, Mari's morning subjects of math and reading were completely sabotaged. Getting her to eat breakfast made her a better student. Another one-minute temper tantrum solution. Of course, don't adults who diet get awfully grumpy as well?

Many children are far more susceptible to tantrums when they are tired, hungry, or sick. The adult should make an evaluation of what and how the child feels and/or how he or she has been affected physically. If appropriate, direct the child to change his or her condition: feed himself or herself, get a drink of juice or water, take a nap, have some quiet time.

> Many children are far more susceptible to tantrums when they are tired, hungry, or sick.

- If necessary, take medical measures to help a child deal with illness symptoms and recover.
- Learn how the child normally acts when well rested versus being tired. Once aware of normal behavior, then indications of getting tired will be easy to recognize.
- Ideally, you can gradually train the child to be self-aware of his or her physical condition and learn what to do to take appropriate care of his or her needs.
- Adults' awareness allows recognition of when the situation is too much for the child given his or her physical condition. Then the activity can be adapted to fit the energy level of the children.

4. EMOTIONAL CONDITION/DISRUPTION

People tend to live their lives in a rhythm, which if disrupted causes disrupted behavior. Adults sometimes do not recognize minor disruptions for children: a holiday, a visit from Grandma, a schedule change, someone new in the class, and anything different in the normal routine. The disruption may be otherwise considered exciting or rewarding. A kindergarten teacher told about a little boy who was all over the classroom for the week. She finally asked him what was going on with him. Vibrating with excitement, he said, "I'm going to Disneyland on Saturday!" There may be major disruptions.

> . . . marital separation and divorce, parental illness, physical and/or emotional neglect, or poor quality parenting. Destructive behavior can develop in association with events that occur during the normal course of development. These events might include the birth of a sibling, beginning school, associating with peers, and moving from elementary to junior high school. All of these events have the potential to exacerbate temper tantrums and shift a child's developmental path toward more maladaptive behaviors. (Ollendick & Schroeder, 2003, p. 661)

A journal article, "Relationship Between Specific Adverse Life Events and Psychiatric Disorders"(Tiet et al., 2001), lists adverse life events in the previous year that youth endorsed as a negative.

Seriously sick or injured

Saw crime or accident

Victim of crime, violence, or assault

Serious sickness or injury of a close friend

Death of a close friend

Breakup with boyfriend or girlfriend

Loss of a close friend

Started going to a new school

Family moved

Family member had drug or alcohol problem

Family member had mental or emotional problem

Family member was seriously ill or injured

Someone in the family died

Someone in the family was arrested

Brother or sister left home

Parents argued more than previously

Parental separation

Parental divorce

Got new stepmother or stepfather

One parent was away from
   home more often
Mother or father figure lost job
Negative change in parent's
   financial situation

Parent got a
   new job
Parent got into trouble
   with the law
Parent went to jail

Although those statistics refer to psychiatric disorders, temper tantrums and other acting-out behavior are also ignited by adverse life events or disruptions. As the adults in children's lives, you need to anticipate changes that may be disruptive to the child. You may unintentionally disrupt children. A very creative and spontaneous teacher came up with the greatest activities on the spur of the moment. However, Hassan had a strong need for routine and structure. Although the activity would be enjoyable, developmentally appropriate, highly stimulating, and facilitate learning, Hassan was thrown off rhythm, resulting in acting-out behavior or tantrums. Be aware of how much you like order and structure versus flexibility and spontaneity. Then you can anticipate how you will affect or disrupt children. As you understand individual children, then you can anticipate how they may be affected by unexpected changes or events. If a child tends to be disrupted, inform the child ahead of time of a change or unexpected event. This gives time to acclimate to change. Reassurance that disruption will not be enduring also helps. In addition, sometimes disruptions in the adults' life, such as a parent's schedule change, can resonate through the family and cause children to be disrupted.

Sam was almost five years old. Unexpectedly, he started to have toilet accidents, which he hadn't had since he was three. He completely flipped out into a tantrum when he wet himself. What is especially annoying about a child that old wetting himself or herself? With the older child, the extra clothes to change into don't fit anymore! Remembering the K.I.S.S. principle, we checked first for any developmental issue or factor that could have caused the toilet accidents. Children three years of age or older are usually intellectually, emotionally, and physically able to handle a toileting situation and also have the communication skills to do so. What situation, the next set of potential igniters, might have caused him to wet himself? Not enough toilets or couldn't get to one quickly enough? Nope. Next, considering possible disruptions, the teacher looked for any recent changes in the classroom, such as a new routine or new classmate. Seeing no significant changes in the classroom, his mother was asked, "Is anything different going on in Sam's life? Has anything changed recently at home?" She responded, "No, nothing. Everything is pretty much the same." She paused for a second, "Well, his dad has been gone for a couple of days. But he's been away on business before . . . so that's not really different." His dad had been on business trips when Sam was younger and was not aware of his being gone. This was the disruption that threw Sam off, causing him to wet himself. Another child might have moped, cried, or fought. The teacher called Sam over, bent down, and said, "You kind of miss Dad don't you?" Sam nodded sadly. "Well, he's coming back tonight." Sam started to smile. "If you are missing him a little bit, just come and get a hug to help you feel better. Okay?" Sam nodded in confirmation. "Are you a little sad now? Do you want a hug?" Sam came over and got himself a hug, and then trotted off to play. And no more toilet accidents. A one-minute temper tantrum solution.

Are there people who are stressed, erratic, or somehow different than usual? Has the routine become highly unpredictable, erratic, or momentarily changed? A child may be bothered by something but is unable to directly identify what is bothering him or her. A child may not be aware of his or her reaction to the stress. The child may have vague, uncomfortable, and lingering stress.

> A child may be bothered by something but is unable to directly identify what is bothering him or her.

- When an individual can identify feelings, he or she usually feels a great relief. Expressing it out loud is an assertion that it is okay to have those feelings.
- If appropriate, prompt the child to accept and express his or her feeling or condition from the disruption. "I'm mad!" "I miss my Daddy," "I don't like that!" And validate the child—"You're really mad!" "You must miss your dad."

Direct the child to stabilize the environment, if possible. Otherwise, the teacher may need to alter the classroom environment, if appropriate and relevant. Returning the environment to an original state is often unrealistic and undesirable. A new stability may need to be established.

CHAPTER HIGHLIGHTS

- Since shortage or unavailability of resources may trigger a tantrum, resolution may come from providing the desired resource or socialization in how to share or negotiate resources. This may be developmentally challenging.
- Attention seeking may demand getting one's functional needs met but may also call for attention to serve emotional or psychological needs.

- Children's mood and susceptibility to temper tantrums are affected by being sick, hungry, or tired; thus, prevention or intervention may be providing adequate rest, food, and helping a child get physically healthy.

- When adults are aware of anything, including their own behavior that might disrupt children and ignite temper tantrums, they can act to stabilize the situation or environment.

- When a child has a tantrum, adults should start examining developmental issues and then subsequently situational, physical, and disruption issues in order. Often, these first four perspectives are sufficient to resolve problems.

Temperamental Factors

4

They Were Born That Way!

On the very first day, as the nurse was changing our first daughter's diaper, she said, "How are you doing, little baby?" My daughter gazed at her with open, calm eyes. The nurse exclaimed to us, "What a little sweetheart you have!" I responded, puffing out my chest, "Of course, it's genetic!"

Fast-forward two and a half years. . . . On our second daughter's very first day, another nurse was changing her diaper. She cooed, "Hi sweetie . . . how you doing?" This daughter looked her in the eyes . . . and screamed at the top of her lungs, "Ahhhhh!" I quickly pointed at my wife lying wearily in the bed, and said, "Uh . . . of course, it's genetic!"

5. TEMPERAMENTAL ISSUES—DIDN'T HAVE THE CHANCE TO RUIN HER

I have two wonderful daughters who, from birth, showed different personalities and temperaments. Throughout childhood and now as a young adult, my oldest daughter continues to have a mellow temperament. My other daughter was born with a somewhat more intense temperament. Don't get me wrong . . . she's a wonderful person! However, she has always been our passionate child who feels deeply. This has made her a lot of fun—and sometimes challenging! It must be inborn temperament, because I didn't have the chance to ruin her! She came out that way! Herbert (2003) notes,

> Children's inborn, idiosyncratic characteristics, and their large differences in sensitivity to their environment, make implausible . . . (a) notion of a purely environmental "programming" of the child. Any nurse who has duties in a nursery of newly born babies or any mother who has had several children and can thus compare her babies knows that they differ markedly in temperament from the very beginning. (p. 239)

In a classroom of 20+ children, temperamentally, they come that way. They have been that way from the very beginning for their parents to deal with. And now for you to deal with. This is about temperamental differences but also about hyperactivity a bit and the different ways we look at kids' behavior. In terms of hyperactivity, the $64,000 question is "I got this wild kid! What is going on?" For another child, the question is why is he or she so careful and cautious? For another, how could we help him or her cope with his or her frustration? For still another, why is it so easy when it is so much harder for other kids? Distinguishing temperament is important for understanding that nothing is "wrong" with the individual. Temperamental differences are entirely normal within a range of temperaments and combinations of temperamental traits, resulting in varied yet understandable personalities. Temperament needs to be understood when examining behavior. And temperament absolutely applies to adults as well.

> Temperamental differences are entirely normal within a range of temperaments and combinations of temperamental traits, resulting in varied yet understandable personalities.

AVOIDING MISDIAGNOSIS AND PATHOLOGIZING

Temperament and family systems issues are often two misunderstood areas that can cause significant misdiagnosis and harm to children. Understanding temperament and family systems issues often saves children from being pathologized. For example, guidance derived from a temperamental evaluation helps with active behavior identifying a child as having attention deficit hyperactivity disorder (ADHD). Negative family or classroom dynamics may be understood through temperamental perspectives. Adults falsely assume that the behavior is intentionally defiant, rather than from natural energy and temperament. Adults may not understand how their temperament ignites, exacerbates, and otherwise interacts with children's temperaments. A temperamental evaluation can lead to reduced frustration, acting out, and tantruming. On the other hand, good behavior and calm classrooms may be essentially about a good match among those children and teachers. Or you have a temperamentally easy child who is easy to parent and teach and relatively difficult to ruin! Women often say they can recognize the easy or difficult baby during pregnancy, as the activity level of each child was already evident inside them. Each person is born with a distinct set of temperamental traits, a unique personality. The mix of temperamental traits creates both positive and challenging personalities for people. Adults need to understand their temperament, how it matches up well or poorly with the child, and regulate behavior according to the match or mismatch to make the relationship more successful. Teachers and parents need to look at the "goodness of fit" between a child and the adult. With respect to a poor fit, it becomes the responsibility of the adult to make adjustments. In addition, different cultural values, including different teachers and families, will value or punish various temperamental traits. The question is not "why does he or she behave a certain way when . . . but how does he or she behave when . . . ." Parents, teachers, other adults, and, eventually, peer and media and other cultural factors interplay with temperament but are not the original cause of temperamental characteristics.

> Adults need to understand their temperament, how it matches up well or poorly with the child, and regulate behavior according to the match or mismatch to make the relationship more successful.

TEMPERAMENTAL EVALUATION TRAITS

The Difficult Child by Stanley Turecki (1989) is an excellent resource on temperament. The following temperamental traits from his book are based on the work of Stella Chess and Alexander Thomas (1996), whose New York Longitudinal Study presents their research that began in 1956. Being high, medium, or low in any trait is not implicitly good or bad. Also, there is not necessarily any absolute scale by which to rate people. A husband rated himself high and his wife medium for the activity-level trait. His wife, on the other hand, rated him medium and herself low in activity. They both agreed that he was higher in the trait than her. What is subjectively high or medium versus low activity levels are not as important as the relative ranking of the different individuals.

1. **Activity level**: How active generally is the child or individual from an early age?

2. **Distractibility**: How easily is the child or individual distracted?

3. **Intensity**: How loud is the child or individual generally, whether happy or unhappy?

4. **Regularity**: How predictable is the child or individual in his or her patterns of sleep, appetite, and bowel habits?

5. **Persistence**: Does the child or individual stay with something he or she likes? How persistent or stubborn is he or she when wanting something?

6. **Sensory threshold**: How does the child or individual react to sensory stimuli: noise, bright lights, colors, smells, pain, warm weather, tastes, the texture and feel of clothes? Is he or she easily bothered? Is he or she easily overstimulated?

7. **Approach/withdrawal**: What is the child or individual's initial response to newness—new places, people, foods, clothes?

8. **Adaptability**: How does the child or individual deal with transition and change?

9. **Mood**: What is the child or individual's basic mood? Do positive or negative reactions predominate?

When the traits for the entire family or group of people are ranked, you can make an evaluation of how well or poorly the temperaments fit each other. Each temperamental trait and the combination of traits create both potential strengths and challenges for individuals and relationships. Young children are often developmentally unable to self-monitor. They have difficulty being self-aware of how their behavior affects other people. In addition, they are also often developmentally unable to self-regulate, to tell themselves what to do to be successful. As the adult, you are responsible for monitoring your children and yourself for how temperament creates problems versus opportunities for them. Regulate the children and yourself to make necessary behavioral choices. While conscientiously monitoring and regulating children, explain to children what you have observed and why you are requiring specific behavior. Educate children to understand their temperaments. Teach children to accentuate strengths from their temperament and to mitigate challenges from the negative aspects.

> Teach children to accentuate strengths from their temperament and to mitigate challenges from the negative aspects.

Children with age-appropriate self-monitoring and self-regulating abilities do well in classrooms. However, problems arise if the classroom requires greater self-monitoring and self-regulating skills than the children possess.

THE COSMIC YARDSTICK

When there is a clear misfit between two members, often the adult, parent, teacher, or a more powerful person asserts that the other person needs to change. In the classic Disney movie *Mary Poppins* (Stevenson, 1964), Mary Poppins pulls out a tape measure in the nursery to measure the two children. She reads from the tape measure, which points out various faults of character. Then she holds it up to herself and proclaims the tape's measure of her: "Mary Poppins, practically perfect in every way!" The cosmic yardstick is how we measure ourselves and other people's character. However, each person's cosmic yardstick often turns out to be a very personal yardstick of morality and values, inappropriately applied to others without regard to different life experiences. For example, if you can endure and enjoy a very high degree of stimulation and activity, you may assume that another person should have an equivalently high sensory threshold. Added stimulation becomes an unintentional disrespectful provocation that overwhelms the other person. "Why are you doing this to me?" The rhetorical question is really an accusation, because the implicit answer is always, ". . . because you don't care for me or respect me, you jerk!" People are not doing anything to the other person but expressing their personalities. With discovery, understanding, and acceptance, people are able to self-monitor and self-regulate, and, with permission, cross-monitor and cross-regulate each other's sensitivities and behavior. A person should not assume that others handle the same level of stimulation that he or she can. The second person should not assume that the first person is trying to stress him or her purposely. One may practice restraint out of respect for how activity overwhelms the other person. The other person could extend or stretch to tolerate greater energy and stimulation. The degree of tolerance for sensory stimulation is a critical trait for looking at children's behavior, especially temper tantrums. A classroom full of children is an inherently highly stimulating environment, with energies bouncing off of each other. Teachers need to be aware that children get overstimulated easily and how they react. They are not acting crazy "at" you to make you crazy, too!

TEMPERAMENTAL FACTORS AFFECTING TANTRUMS

- Temperamental challenges, in general, may have overwhelmed efforts to suppress the energy of the tantrum.
- Low sensory threshold is the most challenging temperament trait leading to tantrums. A child who is unable to tolerate much

sensory stimulation overloads quickly, setting up the potential to tantrum.

- High activity, high distractibility, and high approach to new situations tend to aggravate low sensory threshold further by bringing on even more stimulation. Adding high intensity in expressing feelings (perhaps especially anger or distress), the tantrum becomes explosive.

- Low distractibility in itself defeats the often-recommended tantrum solution or intervention of distraction. Coffey and Brumback note that "parents who 'distract' their children during temper tantrums will be successful with highly distractible children, but not with children who have low distractibility. Children with low distractibility do not seem to hear when they are spoken to if they are involved in their favorite activities" (Coffey & Brumback, 1998, p. 121).

A child who is unable to tolerate much sensory stimulation overloads quickly, setting up the potential to tantrum.

- Controlling (reducing) stimulation for a child with a low sensory threshold is a logical approach to prevent tantrums. Once the tantrum is active, the validation approach that is described in a later section on upset tantrums is recommended.

- A person with high intensity will tantrum with high intensity. A person with low intensity will tantrum with low intensity. The low-intensity person may be just as upset or frustrated, but his or her tantrums may be ignored, as other people assume that it is not a big deal. On the other hand, a high-intensity person may have a minor upset, but because he or she expresses all problems loudly and passionately, he or she may draw more adult attention and energy, including more repercussions than necessary.

- High-adaptability individuals can be extremely upset. However, they may figure out a way to deal with the upset and self-soothe, without adults even realizing there ever was an issue because they had not acted out or thrown a tantrum.

- A high-persistence individual in a manipulative tantrum will stay in tantrum mode much longer. "Children with long attention spans and persistence . . . when these children start a temper tantrum, it is difficult to stop it" (Coffey & Brumback, 1998, p. 121).

- A low-persistence individual may start to tantrum and then slide quickly into hopelessness if his or her behavior doesn't draw immediate attention.

Through understanding temperament, adults can predict children's behavior and, as a result, make changes in management to help them be more successful. Many children are poor fits for some teachers and classrooms while doing extremely well with other teachers and class-rooms. Classrooms always have a mix of temperaments: active children, distractible ones, the slow-to-warm-up ones, the focused kids, the mellow kids, the quiet ones, the gung ho types, and so forth. Teachers won't usu-ally get a homogeneous group of the focused and mellow children. Is there a plan for the active children? A plan for the distractible children? Feeling you shouldn't have to deal with them becomes irrelevant, because you have to deal with them. Temperamentally challenged young children cannot self-monitor or self-regulate easily. They have to be guided by aware and knowledgeable adults. Adults who do not under-stand or accept temperamental theory will insist that the child self-mon-itor and self-regulate. Both adults and children become frustrated and often tantrum as they fail. Then the adults will pathologize the child as "bad."

THE TEMPERAMENTALLY DIFFICULT CHILD

Very active—may be hyperactive. Has been a very happy kid up until recently. His overall mood has turned more negative since the beginning of the first grade (now in third grade). Gets overstimulated easily when there is a lot of noise and activity and doesn't handle it well at all. Gets wild and bothered. Won't give up. Keeps on pushing; won't take "no" for an answer. Can't come up with alternatives when he is frustrated. Gets increasingly upset. Starts throwing tantrums, lashing out at anyone around, "It's your fault! You're mean! I hate you! I wish you weren't my mother. I want to live with my father! You don't care about me!"

Charlie has been criticized over and over for not sitting still, for touching things, for blurting out and interrupting others, for his tantrums, for get-ting into fights at school, for not listening, for not behaving, and so on and so forth. As a result, his self-esteem has suffered a lot. He does not see him-self as a good kid; instead, he thinks he can't be a good kid. He has tried so hard but sees himself as a failure. He alternates between being depressed, being angry, and being excited and happy.

Depending on the mix of nine temperamental traits, the temperament of an individual gives him or her strengths and challenges. Three com-mon temperamental profiles are

The Easy Child, who is very adaptable and handles stress and life fairly easily without much difficulty;

The Slow-to-Warm-Up Child, who eventually does adapt and do well, but needs time to get acclimated, make transitions, and adjust; and

The Difficult Child, who is the most challenging and the most challenged child.

> [Ten] percent were "difficult," or to use an unkind but heartfelt description used by many other research participants, "mother-killers" . . . identified [by] a cluster of temperamental traits that typified the difficult children. The first is the predominance of intense reactions. These children shriek more frequently than they whine, give belly laughs more often than smile. They will express their disappointment not with a whimper, but a bang. Frustration characteristically produces a violent tantrum. Pleasure is also expressed loudly, often with jumping, clapping and running about. (Herbert, 2003, pp. 240–241)

The Temperamentally Difficult Child's profile ends up being fairly typical of, in *DSM-IV* (psychological disorder) terminology, "attention deficit hyperactivity disorder," or being hyperactive (American Psychiatric Association, 1994). Individual traits may be positive or negative depending on what is going on in a particular situation. Charlie has the following trait characteristics that combine to create dynamics to make them particularly challenging:

- High activity level
- High approach
- High distractibility
- Low sensory threshold
- High intensity
- Low adaptability
- High persistence

The combination of seven of nine traits makes Charlie the classic hyperactive child—also known as the difficult child or the wild child . . . or the curse of the classroom! The key trait is his low sensory threshold. He gets overstimulated easily, which his other traits of high activity, high approach to new things, and high distractibility exacerbate by causing excessive stimulation. His high-intensity reaction means he gets very upset. His high persistence causes him to continue acting out despite his failure at solving problems; and his low adaptability prevents him from trying alternative approaches that may be more effective. Together, high persistence and low adaptability worsen his problems. Adults need to monitor him and regulate him toward more appropriate behavior and to teach him to self-monitor and self-regulate. Adults need to be his resource because he is not adaptable. Adults need to tell him how to reduce and avoid overstimulation, to stay focused, to eliminate unsuccessful behavior rather than persist at it, to be more cautious in new situations, and to make adjustments in behavior. If adults are adaptable or resourceful and persistent, they keep working with Charlie until he internalizes his challenges and compensations to be successful on his own. It will take some work but will lead to the successful application of the one-minute temper tantrum solution. However, the low-adaptability adult will have difficult providing resources for challenged children. The low-adaptability adult may either persist with ineffective interventions or give up trying. His or her frustration can perpetuate an ongoing reciprocal tantrum process with a difficult child. Adults who do not understand their own temperaments or their children's temperament tend to be more critical, angrier, more frustrated, less effective, and tend to feel more overwhelmed by classroom management and discipline. They are more likely to pathologize children and/or themselves. Conversely, adults who understand both their and children's personalities tend to

- be less surprised by behavior
- be more effective in predicting and preventing negative behavior
- be more supportive of children's emotional needs
- foster greater self-esteem in children
- feel more effective as teachers and parents
- have higher self-esteem

> Adults who do not understand their own temperaments or their children's temperament tend to be more critical, angrier, more frustrated, less effective, and tend to feel more overwhelmed by classroom management and discipline.

Adults and children who are good temperamental matches tend to have less conflict. They find discipline simpler. Teachers and parents and children who are poor temperamental matches tend to have more conflict; relationships can become extremely strained. And both adults and children will throw tantrums as a result. The dynamics of temperamental differences among children and adults affecting behavior and relationships need to be identified and understood for successful interactions. Acceptance by adults of the temperamental differences between them and the children leads to less negative judgment and greater compassion. This becomes the foundation to subsequent successful discipline and successful applications of the one-minute temper tantrum solutions.

CHAPTER HIGHLIGHTS

- Children are born with different temperaments, which predispose them to more or less vulnerability to tantrums. The difficult child is most likely to have behavior problems and to throw temper tantrums.

- Learning about eight temperamental traits allows adults to avoid misdiagnosis and to better monitor and regulate children and their behavior, eventually leading to children self-monitoring and self-regulating themselves.

- People often expect that others will respond to and behave the same way they would, according to their own temperament.

- Low sensory threshold (a limited ability to handle much stress) creates the greatest vulnerability to tantruming. Other temperamental traits can contribute to tantrums or exacerbate them.

- Adults and children with good temperamental matches predict a higher likelihood and successful resolution of problems.

Systemic Factors   **5**

The Savior

Brad was playing with his dinosaurs as Mom and the teacher were talking. Mom mentioned she hadn't been as attentive with Brad's homework the last week because she was involved in the funeral arrangements of a close friend who had died unexpectedly. She began to tear up and her voice quavered as she talked about her deep grief. Suddenly, Brad threw his dinosaurs against the wall. Mom stopped crying immediately and reprimanded Brad.

Unbeknownst to her, Brad had just saved her from her grief. He got into trouble, but he was the savior.

6. ENVIRONMENTAL AND ECOLOGICAL FACTORS

Every child and person operates within multiple systems of people, such as a family or a class or a workplace. Working with children in a classroom in isolation is not realistic or effective. Children come from and go to other communities: home, school, neighborhood, mall, park, worlds of literature, the media world, and more. Some adults would like their home or classroom to be like playing only with peaceful Barney the purple dinosaur, in gentle Mister Rogers' neighborhood, at the "happiest place on earth," and encased in an impenetrable glass globe away from the harshness of the "real world." Education, development, and discipline, however, are preparation for the real world, where it may not be peaceful, gentle, or happy. Neither home nor the classroom is the real world, but they are the first transitional worlds or communities to guide children into adult worlds. Challenges occur when these worlds collide. The first challenge is often between home and classroom.

Behaviors and attitudes cross among the multiple systems. The National Association for the Education of Young Children (2007) reports:

Development and learning occur in and are influenced by multiple social and cultural contexts. . . . An ecological model for understanding human development [and] children's development is best understood within the sociocultural context of the family, educational setting, community, and broader society. These various contexts are interrelated, and all have an impact on the developing child.

Through coordinating all influential systems, colliding worlds best serve children's development and learning. The school and home partnership serves students in many realms.

Students with involved parents are more likely to

- Earn higher grades and test scores, and enroll in higher-level programs;
- Be promoted, pass their classes, and earn credits;
- Attend school regularly;
- Have better social skills, show improved behavior, and adapt well to school; and
- Graduate and go on to postsecondary education.

In addition, Editorial Projects in Education (2004) reports,

Working to include parents is particularly important as students grow older, and in schools with high concentrations of poor and minority students. . . . When schools, families, and community groups work together to support learning, children tend to do better.

Although some educators may ignore the interrelatedness of the home and school behavior, the reciprocal influences are very powerful. Sometimes an out-of-control child comes from an out-of-control family or is in a out-of-control classroom. The behaviors, the communication style, and the health and stability (or lack thereof) of the system can cause significant emotional, psychological, and behavioral harm to individuals. Behaviors may be modeled and promoted in the system.

A quick temper usually comes from growing up with a quick-tempered adult. The adult's behavior is passed on to the child by way of example. Sometimes a child is taught to be aggressive directly by parents. . . . This child learns that throwing temper tantrums is an effective way to get what is wanted. As the tendency to throw a temper tantrum continues into adult life, it becomes self-defeating.

Sometimes having a quick temper helps a child survive a harsh environment or a social setting where such a temper is valuable. (Peurifoy, 2005, p. 264)

Without the system becoming more stable and healthy, the troubled child struggles to get better. If the child's home or classroom has erratic rules, arbitrary discipline, moody or emotionally unavailable adults, other problematic members, unstable schedules and structures, ineffective communication, triangulation (taking sides), secrets, unstable roles and boundaries, and so forth, the child may act out, be moody, and have major tantrums, among many other possibilities. The health or stability of the most powerful members of the system—normally the parents or the teachers—determines health in a system. If adults react appropriately, children respond with functional behavior. For example,

> . . . an indulgent mother [does] not give a begging and whiny son a breath mint. As the boy begins to have a screaming, yelling, breath-holding tantrum, the mother shows signs of giving in . . . [but] the mother [does] not . . . give in. When discovering that her son eventually stops his tantrum, the mother realizes she has some control over her ill-tempered child, which results in the cessation of daily tantrums at home. (Cheng & Myers, 2005, p. 465)

Emotionally stable adults respond more appropriately to children's behaviors. Adults are more likely to be indulgent if they had negative experiences with feeling either deprived or spoiled during their own childhood. They may fear that their children will be as disappointed or hurt as they had been when they did not receive support or things they needed or wanted in their childhood. They could also feel that their children cannot handle wanting something and having to wait for it, because when they were children, they had not experienced wanting or waiting for a long time—it had been intolerable to want and wait, and because of their parents' immediate indulgence, they never discovered that it could be tolerated. Negative family experiences may also lead to adults who respond characteristically as what O'Leary, Slep, and Reid (1999) call "overreactive parents."

> [C]hildren readily imitate the aggressive behavior of adults. Many overreactive parenting behaviors, such as verbal and physical aggression, arguing, and overt expressions of anger, have direct parallels among the externalizing items . . . parents cease behaving in ways children do not like (e.g., stop overreacting) when children act out, which negatively reinforces externalizing

behaviors. In this case, overreactivity is a marker or necessary condition, but the cessation of overreactivity is the functional or causal parenting behavior. . . . The confirmation of our hypotheses about the stability and effects of mothers' overreactivity points to the importance of identifying predictors of overreactive discipline. (p. 339)

Their findings regarding mothers can be extrapolated to teachers in the classroom. O'Leary et al. (1999) further add, "In this sample, mothers' depressive symptomotology and marital discord were correlated with overreactivity toward their girls and boys, respectively" (p. 339). Unhealthy or unstable individuals tend to create unhealthy or unstable environments, be they households, classrooms, or work situations for others. Unhealthy or unstable individuals create systems in which the children's needs are frustrated, causing acting out and tantrums. Prevention of tantrums comes from addressing the illness of the system and of the powerful members of the system. Despite some educators' discomfort in working with parents (and vice versa), "Changing outcomes for children and youth with serious emotional disturbances and their families . . . requires persistent collaboration with families" (Woodruff et al., 1998, p. 103).

> If the child's home or classroom has erratic rules, arbitrary discipline, moody or emotionally unavailable adults, other problematic members, unstable schedules and structures, ineffective communication, triangulation (taking sides), secrets, unstable roles and boundaries, and so forth, the child may act out, be moody, and have major tantrums, among many other possibilities.

THE CLASSIC FUNCTIONAL SYSTEM

Imagine a platter representing the family system or classroom balanced on a point. In the middle of the platter stand the leaders. In the classic nuclear family, it would be two parents. In a classroom, it would be the teacher and perhaps an aide. In other family models, it could be a single parent, a pair of same-sex parents, a grandmother, uncle, or other extended family member, a foster parent, and so forth. There needs to be someone or some leadership who is centered in the system, and is emotionally, spiritually, intellectually, and (usually) physically healthy and stable for the system. Like the child in the middle of a seesaw, the leaders shift attention and resources this or that way to keep balance. They react but not overreact. The stable-centered parents or teachers need to be prepared and knowledgeable about development and childhood issues. If someone is sad, the centered adults can shift attention and energy toward that person to meet his or her needs. If high energy needs expression, the centered adults provide an active outlet in sports or dance. If a child struggles in math, tutoring or additional support is provided. If the noise and energy level in the house or classroom has gotten out of hand on a rainy day, the centered adults direct children to more appropriate behaviors. The need for adults to be capable, healthy, and responsible becomes greater with greater challenges such as with tantrums, difficult children, and children with special needs.

> In the case of difficult children the handling problem is present from the onset. The parents must cope with the child's irregularity and the slowness with which he adapts in order to establish conformity to the family's rules of living. If the parents are inconsistent, impatient or punitive in their handling of the child, he is much more likely to react negatively than other children are. Only by exceptionally objective, consistent treatment, taking full account of the child's temperament can he be brought to get along easily with others and to learn appropriate behavior. This may take a long time, but with skilful handling such children do learn the rules and function well. . . . (Thomas, Chess, & Birch, 1970, ¶ 17)

Born into a functional family or assigned to a functional classroom, difficult children or children with special needs may otherwise thrive. Centered adults respond to and provide support for their needs and allow the children to be children. An American ideal is for a child to enjoy being a child, to enjoy the developmental process, to play and explore, to grow and develop. In many societies, including poorer communities or families in America, children are not allowed the luxury of being a child in this sense. They are active members of the family's economy.

THE CLASSIC DYSFUNCTIONAL SYSTEM

Temperamentally difficult children or other children with demanding conditions, when they are unfortunate to have been born into a dysfunctional family, often suffer the worst consequences. Erratic adults miss their needs, and children become increasing anxious. A dysfunctional family may be highly toxic and identifiable to outsiders, if they are able to see inside the home. Often, the dysfunction is hidden. Children in such systems suffer major negative consequences. For example,

> Virtually all children living in a home where one parent assaults and terrorizes the other are aware of the violence. . . . Studies show that such role models perpetuate violence into the next

generation. . . . Children who witness abuse frequently evidence behavioral, somatic and emotional problems similar to those experienced by physically abused children. . . . Older boys tend to become aggressive, fighting with siblings and schoolmates and have temper tantrums. Girls are more likely to become passive, clinging and withdrawn, and to suffer low self-esteem. (Hart, 1992, p. 33)

> Temperamentally difficult children or other children with demanding conditions, when they are unfortunate to have been born into a dysfunctional family, often suffer the worst consequences.

However, although dysfunctional systems may appear innocuous to others, powerful dynamics create painful stereotyped survival mechanisms and roles. The classic dysfunctional system (e.g., the alcoholic family system) needs the children to maintain functioning of the classroom or family. Adults, instead of being centered in the platter, are off center. One may be emotionally, psychologically, or chemically (drugs or alcohol) "out there" and unable to provide balancing in response to children's needs. Other issues, particularly workaholism or codependent behavior, may appear positive but are also harmful. With two adults, the other adult has to be overresponsible to deal with the irresponsible behavior of the first. The overresponsible adult has to anticipate how the irresponsible adult will screw up. Ironically, it is the dedication of the second adult that allows the first adult to be irresponsible. As long as the system is maintained, although at great cost to everyone, the irresponsible adult does not have to suffer the complete consequences of his or her actions. The family or classroom keeps functioning, but at great stress and cost to everyone. Sometimes, instead of a second adult, it is a child who maintains the balance of the system. Sometimes, multiple children, rather than a single child, maintain the balance.

The Hero

In a dysfunctional system, a very common role is the role of the Hero or the responsible one. This child makes sure that the daily life of the household or classroom goes on. He or she makes lunches and cleans at home or straightens the bookshelf and hangs up coats in the classroom. The Hero child is often well respected. Often this child is considered to be an achiever and a little "grownup" or a little "teacher," but unfortunately is not allowed to be a child with a real sense of self-worth. This child is not likely to tantrum frequently but may secretly feel unfulfilled and depressed.

The Nurturer

The Nurturer takes care of the emotional needs of the family: soothing the sad child, being caring and vigilant about everyone and their feelings. Some grow up to be professional nurturers, such as teachers, therapists, social workers, nurses, and so forth. Gender stereotypes and culture promote this role even more for females. Sweet, kind, and considerate, the Nurturer nurtures everyone, but doesn't nurture his or her own emotional needs. The unnurtured Nurturer and the Hero may eventually tantrum but in self-destructive ways, such as in overeating, hypervigilance, and self-medication.

The Lost Child

Often times, there is a Lost Child in such a family. The Lost Child somehow realizes that this family cannot meet his or her emotional needs and decides to no longer risk being disappointed. He or she gives up hope and spends his or her energy becoming invisible as the safest and surest method for survival. The Lost Child will exist in classrooms, at work, and other places, but be barely noticed. The Lost Child may not tantrum overtly or cause problems because that brings unwanted attention. Quietly and desperately depressed, if he or she tantrums, it will be a helpless tantrum.

The Distracters

In the dysfunctional family, tension inevitability increases, causing painful eruptions. The Distracter will try to save the family through distraction. The distracting Mascot is often the sunshine of the family, just about perfect. This family, with so much pain and dysfunction, has a powerful need to have some sunshine, and the Mascot is it. The Mascot cannot, however, mess up ever, or else the sunshine of the entire family will be eclipsed. The Mascot will seek out situations and people who find him or her special and heap praise on him or her. However, in the real world, not everyone will find him or her adorable. When Mascots come to the classroom, they expect to be special there as well but may be rejected and devastated. Tantrums may result from the lack of special treatment. Many great comedians may have been distracting clowns in their families. As children in painfully dysfunctional families, they had the wit to be funny, but more than that, they had to be funny to distract the family from the pain of dysfunctionality. When the tension rises to an unbearable level, release of tension from a well-spoken joke or wisecrack is greatly welcome. On the other hand, the Clown will keep on making wisecracks even when it is not welcome or needed. Deep dark inner pain still eats at them. Tantrums may erupt when the inner pain becomes intolerable.

The Rebel

Then there are the Scapegoats . . . the Rebels . . . the Bad Ones. Every one of the other roles, except for the Lost Child, functions to save the system from its pain. The Rebel tries to save the family or classroom from its pain by acting out, being bad, and failing. In a dysfunctional system, another crisis is inevitable. The checks start bouncing. Child Protective Services shows up. The parent or teacher loses it and tantrums. It gets scarier for the children as they fear that the system will self-destruct. Each of them except for the Lost Child activates their roles to save the family or classroom. The Rebel creates an alternative crisis by getting into a fight or throwing a tantrum. The Rebel's behavior draws the couple from their relationship crisis as a dysfunctional couple and forces them to take the role of being parents. They show up together at school to meet with the teacher. Attention now focused on the Rebel, the implicit danger that the family feels subsides. All the children relax. The family has been saved. In a classroom, a teacher's growing frustration and anger puts the entire classroom on edge. The Rebel saves classmates by acting out or tantruming to draw the teacher's rage to himself or herself. Unfortunately, the Rebel's reputation and self-esteem are also diminished. The Rebel feels compelled to get into trouble and sacrifice himself or herself for the family or classroom. As the crisis fades, the Rebel's behavior improves, everyone returns to normal, and the tension gradually begins to rise again. When it reaches the crisis point again, the Rebel looks for another fight, throws another tantrum . . . or if older, acts out with drugs or alcohol or sexual or delinquent behavior. Or another child takes a turn as the Rebel. Or the Rebel may realize what the Lost Child figured out a long time ago—that there was nothing he or she could really do, and say, "The heck with this, I am outta here!" Like the other roles, the Rebel may continue with his or her personality and behavior pattern throughout life.

> The Rebel tries to save the family or classroom from its pain by acting out, being bad, and failing. In a dysfunctional system, another crisis is inevitable.

BALANCING THE INNER HERO, NURTURER, LOST CHILD, THE DISTRACTERS (MASCOT AND CLOWN), AND THE REBEL

None of these roles is negative per se. Clowns, at the right time, like Heroes and Nurturers, can be very positive elements in the system. Danger occurs when the role is constant and without discrimination. The Hero always fixes and the Nurturer always nurtures whether or not there is any need. And the Clown keeps on with the wisecracks even when they're disruptive. The Lost Child stays invisible although it costs him or her something needed. The Rebel sometimes draws energy away from other members who need it. On the other hand, the Rebel is the one who is most likely to fight back, to refuse to accept the status quo. And in the dysfunctional family, the status quo stinks! In society, Rebels often provide the impetus for important social change. These roles, in balance, can be part of an overall healthy personality. The ability to judiciously choose to activate each role at appropriate times results in a healthy personality and successful social interaction and relationships. These roles become dysfunctional when the individual doesn't correctly choose appropriate role choices and when the individual cannot access different roles as needed.

> The ability to judiciously choose to activate each role at appropriate times results in a healthy personality and successful social interaction and relationships.

Does a child get stuck into one of these roles? Were or are you still stuck in one of these roles? In some systems, individuals rotate through these roles, each taking a turn as the Hero or Nurturer or even the Rebel. If you noticed a child rotating through roles, it may be a good thing! An angry tantrum from an otherwise meek child may be encouraged and be encouraging! A child needs support as he or she experiments with different roles. Help him or her recognize both the positive and the negative consequences of being in particular roles. If, on the other hand, a child stays in one role, including the ostensibly good roles of Hero or Nurturer, then it is important to examine the overall family or classroom dynamics and system. See if the role serves the system at a cost to individual emotional and psychological health. Accumulated cost for an individual may result in subsequent tantrums. Disciplining to change behavior that comes from role requirements may not address the underlying issues that cause both the role and behavior. Children's so-called bad behavior may be their attempt to save their family or classroom from its pain. Then it becomes important to find out what the family or classroom needs to be saved from. That may take more than one minute, but one minute of communication or parent–teacher interaction may lead to freeing a child stuck in a dysfunctional role. One minute of examination may lead you to getting unstuck in understanding the persistence of a child's behavior and tantruming.

One minute of self-reflection may also free you from your old role(s) that affect your propensity to get frustrated, act out, or tantrum. Perhaps, your tantrums or other behavior is from being tired of being the nice Nurturer! Perhaps, your inner Rebel needs permission. One of my female clients, a long-term Nurturer, likes to contemplate letting her inner Xena (from the television series *Xena: Warrior Princess*) out to wreak some havoc on the toxic bad guys and evil castles of her life! We'd laugh, imagining her as the actress Lucy Lawless dressed up and armed with her sword. Then we would consider how being nice has often disempowered and frustrated her and how to use some of her untapped powerful energy to have a better life. She had always repressed her Rebel, her inner Xena, to be the Nurturer, the "good girl." Loaded with years of frustration and anger, she tantrumed within herself and at others. Finding her Xena and balancing her with her other roles helped my client grow and take firmer charge of her life. For her, Xena the Warrior Princess was a one-minute temper tantrum solution!

CHAPTER HIGHLIGHTS

- Children experience school as a transitional community between the home community, which is nurturing, and later communities that are often more demanding.
- Stable leadership from adults creates functional families and systems that are responsive and able to meet the needs of all members.
- Overreactive adults and dysfunctional systems produce children with behaviors that are often problematic in the classroom, and they are less able to support children with challenges.
- A dysfunctional classroom or family system needs the children to maintain functioning of the classroom or family. As a result, the classroom or family fails to meet children's needs. This becomes especially problematic for children who are difficult or have special needs.
- Children can get stuck in stereotypical roles in dysfunctional families. Access and balance among the roles promotes healthy individuals. The role of the Rebel is most likely to present obvious tantrums.

Specific or Specialized Factors and Moral Factors

6

Try Harder

Can you recognize the opening lines from a children's classic and name the book?

The snu bip uot shiue.
It mas too met to dlay.
So me sat iu the honse
All that colq, colb, met bay.

7. SPECIFIC OR SPECIALIZED FACTORS

There may be something unusual or different about a child. Parents fear that some distinctive aspect about their children may mean there is something "wrong" about their children. Some parents or teachers are hypervigilant and even paranoid, and they see issues where there are none. Other parents or teachers may be so fearful of discovering something disturbing or overwhelming that they ignore clear signals that the child needs special assistance. Attention deficit hyperactivity disorder (ADHD), autism, and learning disabilities may be important issues. Diagnosis of a specific or specialized factor or condition can be intimidating, as people feel that it is beyond their ability to handle or endure addressing it—or they may fear that their children cannot handle the challenges of the factor or condition. Warnings such as the following can be useful, prejudicial, and/or terrifying:

> Drug-exposed infants have abnormal motor development, including tremors in their arms and hands as they reach for objects, and

unusual muscle tone reflexes, or movement patterns. As toddlers and preschoolers, many of these children are easily frustrated and distracted, exhibit frequent temper tantrums, head banging, and have difficulty processing information. (Jackson, 1993, p. 20)

ADD children often exhibit aggressiveness or stubbornness and are prone to temper tantrums. . . . (U.S. Congress, Office of Technology Assessment, 1986, p. 40)

Deep, emotional turmoil in children can be revealed by the combination of common physical symptoms of distress; such as, intermittent and selective stuttering, sleep walking and talking, nightmares, nervous facial and upper body ticks, nose-bleeds, high-pitched nervous laughter, bed-wetting (enuresis) including daytime incontinence. Behavioral symptoms may include expressive dirty and angry language, being loud, throwing things and having tantrums. Other not so easily recognized symptoms which may, however, signify anger or calling for help are eating disorders, somatic complaints such as irritable bowel syndrome, and post traumatic stress disorder. . . . (Pollard, 2002, p. 78)

There may be medical, neurological, or other organic issues that are difficult to understand. Can children "grow out" of the challenges from prenatal exposure, high energy, difficulty socializing, or some other issue? Or will social and emotional damage occur despite growing out of it or while growing out of it? Adults need to be sensitive and vigilant without becoming hypersensitive and hypervigilant regarding complex issues in children. Something being terribly wrong may be indicated by tantrums and other behavior. Neurological conditions, physical and sexual abuse, and other profound influences are not to be dismissed out of hand when children act out. Careful assessment must be taken with such diagnoses both because of potential harm suffered and potential stigma attached to everyone involved. However, both parents and professionals can sensationalize a transitory or minor upset completely out of proportion because sufficient information had not been discovered. Simpler theories or factors should be considered first. Many people jump to more sensational levels of diagnosis inappropriately. The first six sets of factors, issues, or theories presented in this book, from development to temperament, may help resolve most concerns. They may otherwise

> Adults need to be sensitive and vigilant without becoming hypersensitive and hypervigilant regarding complex issues in children.

indicate when more advanced levels of assessment are necessary. All relevant factors—the simpler and the more complex, and how they function interactively—need to be considered. This chapter introduces some specific or specialized factors or conditions but cannot do so comprehensively.

TIME, ATTENTION, AND ENERGY DEMANDS AND EFFECTS

Children with disabilities, special conditions, or challenges require a disproportionate amount of time, attention, and energy of the parents, the siblings, and the family as a whole. They also require disproportionate time, attention, and energy of teachers. Some children may require specialized education, training, resources, and equipment. Some parents will not inform teachers about a prior autistic spectrum, hyperactive, or other important diagnosis. Sometimes, parents are not cognizant enough of their children's conditions to accurately or sufficiently inform teachers. Any behavior or tantrum can be significantly more difficult to handle if there are unidentified complicating conditions. Teachers often identify such students only after they start taking up a lot of energy and focus. There is often a vicious circle of wear and tear on the parents and family or teachers and classroom. Feeling bewildered and inadequate to meet a child's special needs, adults suffer a variety of experiences: depression, guilt, embarrassment, lack of satisfaction, isolation, overinvolvement, anger, exhaustion, and futility. The classroom teacher also may feel isolated dealing with challenging children. And there's still the need to meet standards! Conscientious parents and teachers work extremely hard at raising and teaching these children but are often not acknowledged for their efforts. Others may seem sympathetic but also may be critical and not appreciative of what it takes. People may criticize the front-line adults for not trying hard enough, not caring, or being lazy.

> Feeling bewildered and inadequate to meet a child's special needs, adults suffer a variety of experiences: depression, guilt, embarrassment, lack of satisfaction, isolation, overinvolvement, anger, exhaustion, and futility.

PROCESSING DIFFICULTIES AND DIFFERENCES

Among the most common children with specific or specialized issues that teachers encounter are children with learning disabilities (also commonly referred to as learning disorders) or those who are considered learning different. In this book, I use the acronym "LDs" for all of these terms. Many LD children are mainstreamed with or without diagnosis of a LD. These LD children process, integrate, and retrieve information differently and/or have weaknesses in their processing, integration, and retrieval mechanisms. Individuals do not grow out of LDs. The usual definition of a *learning disability* is a substantial difference between a child's academic performance and what is expected at his or her age. LDs include deficits in visual perception, linguistic processes, auditory processes, attention, and memory. Frustration and failure may lead to behavioral problems or tantrums.

Jules has an undiagnosed LD, which creates difficulty for him in distinguishing the differences in letters that are vertical and/or horizontal "mirrors" of each other: "c," "u," and "n"; "b," "d," "p," and "q"; "m" and "w"; "M" and "W"; and "Z" and "N." As he struggles, the teacher tries to be patient while the other students in the classroom are not. This is the quote from the beginning of the chapter: If you didn't figure it out before, do so now. You don't get to quit. That is not acceptable! If this feels demanding, remember that children, especially LD children, don't get to opt out of requests by adults if these tasks are hard or frustrating.

> The snu bip uot shiue.
> It mas too met to dlay.
> So me sat iu the honse
> All that colq, colb, met bay.

The following is how Jules, a dyslexic child, struggles through deciphering the four simple lines of 23 words. To Jules, each of the underlined letters could be two, three, or more letters because of the difficulty identifying letters that "mirror" each other. With each guess of what letter it may be, Jules has to pause and check if it makes a word he recognizes and also if it makes any sense in the sentence. Each word or cluster of letters in the parenthesis below require that check.

> **The** (snu? snn? suu? suu? sun?) *sun* . . . (bip? bid? biq? diq? dip? diq? pip? pid? piq? qiq? qip? qiq? did?) *did* . . . (uot? not?) *not* . . . (shiue? shine?) **shine** . . . It (mas? was?) **was** . . . **too** (met? wet?) *wet* . . . **to** (dlay? blay? qlay? play?) *play* . . . **So** (me? we?) *we* . . . sat (iu? in?) *in* . . . **the** (hones? house?) **house** . . . **All that** (uolq, colb? uolb, colp? uolp, colb? colq, uolb? colb, uolp? colp, uolb? cold?) *cold* . . . , *cold*, (met? wet?) **wet** . . . (bay? qay? pay? day?) *day* . . .

There were over 50 letter clusters to go through to figure out 23 words. Jules has to take out the false starts and incorrect deciphering, and turn every letter the right direction. Eventually, if he hadn't given up, Jules would discover that the paragraph reads,

> The sun did not shine.
> It was too wet to play.
> So we sat in the house
> All that cold, cold, wet day.

It's the opening paragraph from the classic Dr. Seuss book, *The Cat in the Hat.* The second page has lines of 43 more words. There are 59 other pages, but only 41 of them have words. And how many clusters of letters are there to go through to find out what the words are? Jules, who has tried so hard to please the teacher and to keep up with the other children, has failed. The teacher's frustration and impatience becomes punishing. Unable to please, Jules decides no longer to try. He was punished for trying and becomes sullen and resentful, a silent seething tantrum.

MISDIAGNOSED—COMPENSATION: TRY DIFFERENTLY, *NOT* HARDER!

LD children are often misdiagnosed as mentally deficient or resistant to learning. They are often criticized for not paying attention, being lazy, and are constantly told to try harder. Adults often think they don't care or are being defiant. LD children try very hard to please their parents and teachers and be accepted by other children. As they try and fail over and over, adults and other children stigmatize LD children as being stupid. Worse, they believe themselves to be stupid. Isn't all that what teachers and parents feel after trying so hard? This dynamic reflects a truism of human interactions: individuals you interact with end up making you feel what they are feeling. LD children, children with other specialized issues, and adults who try to support them share many experiences of frustration and failure. As you continue to read about the children's emotional process, remember it often applies to you, too.

> LD children, children with other specialized issues, and adults who try to support them share many experiences of frustration and failure.

Learning or reading disabilities can have destructive emotional effects. Persistent learning failure leads to anguish, embarrassment and frustration. "There is something terrifying about sitting at the back of the class and having somebody ask you questions which you know you will never be able to answer," an adult dyslexic told British actress Susan Hampshire, who is also dyslexic. . . . Nelson Rockefeller, who served as vice president of the United States and governor of the state of New York, recalled, "I was dyslexic, and I still have a hard time reading today. I remember vividly the pain and mortification I felt as a boy of eight when I was assigned to read a short passage of scripture at a community vesper service and did a thoroughly miserable job of it. I know what a dyslexic child goes through . . . the frustration of not being able to do what other children do easily, the humiliation of being thought not too bright when such is not the case at all." (Audiblox, 2007)

Demoralized, LD children become vulnerable to emotional problems, relationship problems, violence, defiance, substance abuse, and, of course, throwing tantrums:

> Behavior problems resulting from their negative experiences are not uncommon in LD youngsters. The strain and the frustration of underachieving can cause them to be reluctant to go to school, to throw temper tantrums before school or in some cases to play truant. Cheating, stealing and experimenting with drugs can also result when children regard themselves as failures. This can worsen as children grow into adolescence. . . . Youngsters with learning disabilities constitute a disproportionately large percentage of adolescent suicides compared with the general adolescent population. [A]nother study, conducted in Ontario, Canada . . . showed that 89 percent of the twenty-seven adolescents who committed suicide had significant deficits in spelling and handwriting that were similar to those of adolescents with LD. (Audiblox, 2007)

> Demoralized, LD children become vulnerable to emotional problems, relationship problems, violence, defiance, substance abuse, and, of course, throwing tantrums.

There have been a significant number of problematic teens with LDs in my therapy practice.

The key to successfully helping LD children comes from first identifying the specific LD; and second, training the child to use compensating techniques and/or skills. Drawing assistance from and using specially trained professional resources is often required and recommended. Some LDs may require expert evaluation and intervention:

> Eight-year-old George was born with hyperacute perceptual sensitivities . . . and specific cognitive weaknesses that became apparent

as he learned to speak. He had trouble coordinating his strong language-based thinking with his intuitive grasp of situations, because of poor functional integration between right and left cerebral hemispheres. He did not have an ear for the "music" of conversation—the nonverbal tones, gestures, and pauses that help people coordinate their utterances with each other. . . . (Trimble, 2001)

George had very difficult temper tantrums complicated by his LD. Most teachers and most therapists would not be experienced or trained to serve the needs of a child like George. A general practitioner may not recognize a nuanced or uncommon condition or be able to provide appropriate terms for a child. Referring to a specialist may be recommended. Not all professionals or programs make precise diagnoses of children with LDs; nor do all offer a specific program to meet children's learning challenges. As a result, over time, children fall farther behind academically and become ever more frustrated, becoming increasingly likely to act out.

BEYOND BALLISTIC

Attention deficit hyperactivity disorder (ADHD) children have "a persistent pattern of inattention and/or hyperactivity-impulsivity that is more frequent and severe than is typically observed in individuals at a comparable level of development" (American Psychiatric Association, 1994, p. 78). Attention deficit disorder (ADD) is similar, but without the hyperactivity. Some people classify ADHD and ADD into the larger spectrum of LDs. Children with ADHD tend to have low self-esteem, mood lability, low frustration tolerance, and temper outbursts:

> Children with hyperreactivity may be very concerned about becoming disorganized and develop rigid routines, compulsions, and stereotypic patterns that help them maintain self-control. . . . They are ways in which the children are trying to monitor and manage their registration and interpretation of sensory input so that they can maintain a level of comfort. . . . Certain types of everyday sensation are actually painful for these children. The sound of a door slamming, unexpected laughter on a television soundtrack, or thunder can be so uncomfortable that the children will do everything they can to avoid experiencing the sensation again. Their rigid, controlling behaviors and rituals are understandable attempts to limit noxious sensory input, or at least to make the input predictable. (Williamson, Anzalone, & Hanft, 2006, p. 159)

Some individuals, misdiagnosed as ADHD, have other disorders, such as pediatric bipolar disorder, Asperger syndrome, depression, and anxiety. In addition, Ashley (2005) notes:

> ADHD rarely exists by itself. More children than not have at least one of the disorders. It is estimated that approximately two thirds of children with ADHD have at least one other mental disorder and as many as ten percent have three or more disorders. Mental disorders are often the norm rather than the exception. . . . The breakdown of coexisting disorders look something like this:
>
> - Second disorder: 66 percent
> - Learning problems: 50 percent
> - Oppositional defiant disorder: 33 percent
> - Anxiety disorder: 25 to 30 percent
> - Conduct disorder: 25 percent
> - Depression: 10 to 30 percent
> - Obsessive-compulsive disorder: 10 to 17 percent
> - Three or more disorders: 10 percent
> - Learning disorders: 10 percent
> - Tourette syndrome: 7 percent (p. 53)

Any specific or specialized condition and issue or interaction among conditions can predispose a child to intensify misbehavior or throw tantrums. Such conditions or issues may also interact with the various underlying issues discussed in this book (e.g., development, situations, disruptions, etc.). Sometimes, there is more to it. Diagnoses and labeling are critical to successful treatment but can also be simplistic and distracting. However, varied diagnoses can be useful. There are children with significant issues that make any tantrum or acting out seem beyond ballistic and approach nuclear fission. Ross W. Greene (2005) lists various diagnoses and collectively calls them "inflexible-explosive" children. He says,

> Their parents quickly discover that strategies that are usually effective for shaping the behavior of other children—such as explaining, reasoning, reassuring, nurturing, redirecting, ignoring, rewarding, and punishing—don't have the same success. . . . Even formal behavior management programs . . . and commonly prescribed medications have not led to satisfactory improvement. . . . Besides oppositional-defiant disorder, children . . . may be diagnosed with any of a variety of psychiatric disorders and learning inefficiencies, including attention-deficit/hyperactivity disorder (ADHD), mood

disorders (bipolar disorder and depression), Tourette's disorder, anxiety disorders (including obsessive-compulsive disorder), language-processing impairments, sensory integration dysfunction, nonverbal learning disabilities, reactive attachment disorder, and even Asperger's disorder. Such children may also be described as having difficult temperaments. . . . These children often seem unable to shift gears and think clearly in the midst of frustration and respond to even simple changes and requests with extreme inflexibility and often verbal or physical aggression. . . . Some scream when they become frustrated but do not swear or become physically or verbally aggressive. . . . Others scream and swear but do not lash out physically . . . becoming inflexible and irrational over the most trivial matters. . . . Still others combine the whole package . . . who reacted to unexpected changes with unimaginable screaming, swearing, and physical violence. . . . (pp. 4–5)

Such children have issues that add to the complexity of their behaviors and of interventions to help them. However, although underlying issues may initially be hidden, mysterious, or difficult to comprehend, they make sense of the child and the behavior. Things never make sense until they make sense! What should work, will work . . . unless there is more to it. In other words, what is illogical and arbitrary becomes logical, and even predictable, once sufficient information and insight has been gained. And sometimes the specific knowledge or insight can lead to a one-minute temper tantrum solution, or at least to a fair amount of prevention and recovery. Seeking such information and insight avoids the last assessment.

> Any specific or specialized condition and issue or interaction among conditions can predispose a child to intensify misbehavior or throw tantrums.

8. MORAL ISSUES

"Bad Boy!" "Bad Girl!" Understanding the other factors helps adults avoid making negative moral judgments against children. Moral rejection is the ultimate negative diagnosis, leading to dismissing the child as being beyond salvation. Unattractive and repulsive personalities, however, may be the consequence of ineffective and misguided parenting and teaching. Henry had repeated trouble, had been suspended, and was on the verge of expulsion. Now in middle school, he had a long history of aggressive behaviors and altercations. He was defiant at times with his teachers and frequently with his mother. His siblings had no problems whatsoever in school. He was considered a "bad kid" or a "bad seed." He was scary when he expressed pride that he could and would hurt other people if they did him wrong. He had not reached developmental milestones (first assessment) as expected during childhood. Henry's early professionals including his pediatrician and preschool and early elementary school teachers did not note it or bring it to his parents' attention. There were particular situations (second assessment) that seemed to be more problematic for him than others. He had more problems when there was a complexity of social cues to examine and respond to. He also acted out more with his mother right before it was time to visit his father—the two of whom had separated several months earlier. There was disruption (fourth assessment) in his weekly schedule moving from one household to another. He was an intense person and very volatile (temperament, the fifth assessment). He had grown up in a chaotic family system (the sixth assessment), witnessing drug abuse by the father and domestic violence against his mother. Now Henry had two family systems: with his stressed single mother and at his grandparents' house with his father. Something was different with his personality and processing (seventh assessment). He had trouble recognizing facial expressions and voice tones to determine whether or not another person was happy or upset. He gave back no nonverbal cues (smiling, nodding, or tipping the head, etc.) to indicate that he understood, agreed with, or integrated anything the other person was communicating.

> Moral rejection is the ultimate negative diagnosis, leading to dismissing the child as being beyond salvation.

Asperger syndrome, which was finally diagnosed by a therapist, was the root of how he became the "Bad Boy." Unable to recognize subtle social cues that his behavior or actions were intrusive or annoying, his continued behavior became extremely negative to his peers. Henry was completely surprised and hurt as people rejected him. He had developed a kind of paranoia and began striking back at the perceived injustices. His parents, due to their own issues, had not been able to note or respond to his issues. The mother, his teachers, and school officials had attempted a multitude of behavioral interventions to no avail. Early recognition of the multiple factors that led to this behavior and attitudes could have directed intervention to teach social cues recognition and appropriate social skills to Henry. This may have precluded the development of his paranoid defense mechanisms and aggressive behavior. Unfortunately, many of the behaviors and paranoid perspectives were now firmly entrenched in his personality and intervention had become much more difficult. The school gave up and worked to expel him.

The eighth and last assessment is a moral assessment. Children are morally judged as unsalvageable, with little if any actual support given anymore. The goal of the school or family becomes maintenance or begrudging tolerance while minimizing disruption or harm to others, until they leave the system. The first seven assessments are critical to avoid this last judgment. Each of the first seven assessments involves logic and logical processes for remedies and interventions. Each also requires adults to be alert and discriminating when interacting with a child. Adults must take responsibility rather than avoid responsibility for guiding the behavior of children. The moral assessment is more than a moral judgment—it is a moral excuse and dismissal. Moral rejection is the one-minute temper tantrum solution to be avoided.

CHAPTER HIGHLIGHTS

- Although some adults are resistant to finding something exceptional about a child, due caution should be maintained before making such a diagnosis because of the ensuing greater concern and complications.
- Children with challenges take more time, attention, and energy and may have significant effects on other children and adults in the home or classroom.
- Children with LDs are often misdiagnosed as stupid and not trying hard. They need to be taught compensations for their learning challenges.
- Children who are labeled bad boys or bad girls with problematic behavior normally have gone through major problems in many areas.
- The eighth assessment of moral corruption is to be avoided because it leads to rejection of a child. The first seven assessments involve logic and logical processes for remedies and interventions and may preclude rejecting a child.

Four Types of Temper Tantrums!

7

Not Always About Power and Control

FOLK AND "EXPERT" REMEDIES FOR TANTRUMS

Ahhhhh! (stomp . . . stomp . . . stomp on the floor). Ahhhhh! (flop . . . flop . . . flop on the floor). Ahhhhh! (bang . . . bang . . . bang fists on the floor).

And the adult does what?

There are many common remedies or folk remedies that are recommended by elders, religious leaders, politicians, self-appointed experts, and professionals who study teaching and parenting processes and child discipline and behavior. You see their proposed remedies all over the Internet and on television. You get suggestions from people who should never be around children! Solutions that would get you arrested for animal abuse if you tried them with a dog. Tried and true methods that encourage you to revert to medieval times but only with a newer version of the rack! And many suggestions encourage ignoring child abuse laws because parents were treated harshly as children as well. There are articles and books. Some are by parents with insight from their challenging children. Some are by parents with out-of-control children or spouses but who now know what they should have done before. Perhaps I should have gotten suggestions from the young couple who had their two-year-old turn their dinner out into an unplanned six-course meal, with "Lovey" alternately screaming, pouting, hitting, and gazing contentedly around the room. No, they didn't have six courses. Just one plate of food that each sat and ate furtively between taking turns walking the kid out of the dining area about twelve times. Odds are that they are following someone's tantrum advice. Some advice is by professionals—professionals who actually work with children! Others are by individuals with dogmatic agendas with remedies based on how children should behave, while ignoring whether or not children actually can behave as mandated. And forget developmentally appropriate practice! Their dogma prescribes effective discipline, without considering the emotional or psychological damage endured. Each remedy is based on some underlying assumption or theory regarding the motivations behind the tantrum. If assumptions are correct, resultant strategies or interventions may be effective. However, if assumptions are incorrect, resultant strategies or interventions may be ineffective, if not also harmful. Common remedies and the underlying assumptions in each include the following:

Indulge the child. One premise is that children are focused solely on acquiring something and that children need to be satisfied because otherwise they will be emotionally damaged by disappointment. Disappointment? Wait until they learn how unspecial they are . . . to the other kids. Resiliency cannot be learned without experiencing disappointment. Children are not that fragile, unless adults teach them to be. That is why it is called "learned helplessness." The other premise for indulging children with what they want is that it is the only way to get them to stop tantruming. "(A) major way that people deal with temper tantrums . . . is to give the children whatever they had the temper tantrums to get. Basically, this teaches kids that if they cry hard enough, or act out sufficiently, they will get whatever they want" (Greene, 1996). This is most likely to happen if adults cannot tolerate either the suffering of a child or cannot suffer the whining, screaming, or conflict with a child. Indulgence develops the sixth sense in addition to the five senses of sight, smell, hearing, taste, and touch—the sense of entitlement! Children and adults develop the expectation that they will be indulged and may become outraged and vindictive if not. Indulging a child who throws a tantrum reinforces inappropriate techniques for power and control. Such self-centered orientation does not serve a community process of needs and collaboration.

> Indulging a child who throws a tantrum reinforces inappropriate techniques for power and control.

Nurture the child. The premise is that nurturing would satisfy the child's need for emotional support and thus put a stop to the tantrum. Children should always be nurtured. They often need adults to provide nurturing so that they can eventually learn how to self-nurture. However, not all tantrums are thrown with the goal of seeking nurture or emotional support. So-called adult support becomes counterproductive if the child is actually seeking greater power and control inappropriately. Or nurturing inadvertently reinforces helplessness in a different tantrum. This creates a sense of victimhood and doom for the child. Adults who have unresolved distress from not being nurtured when younger may nurture compulsively whether a child needs it or not.

Shame the child. The premise is that the child is egocentric and selfishly ignores the needs of other people. It also assumes that the child will stop tantruming to avoid horrible shame inflicted by an adult. Shaming a child may stop the behavior but is dangerous to the self-esteem of the child. Shaming labels a child's needs as inappropriate and selfish. It puts a child's needs as being less important than some other need, such as the teacher's or parent's needs. If an adult wants to stop a tantrum because of the inconvenience or frustration of having to deal with it, he or she may shame the child into stopping. Shaming the child can be devastating to his or her self-esteem, as it ignores the emotional, social, and psychological needs of the child. Shaming is a moral condemnation that continues a cycle of shaming from one generation into the next.

Punish (or threaten or intimidate) the child (sometimes expressed as "not letting them get away with it"). The premise is that the child's desire to avoid punishment is stronger than any need he or she may be expressing through the tantrum. This is a very dangerous assumption. If a tantrum is an expression of the internal emotional process of a child, punishing these natural motivations denies the child's basic human energy. Sometimes, these energies are so important and powerful that they supersede the desire to avoid punishment. This can create a child who continues the misbehavior despite being punished and who becomes immune to punishment. This is discussed at length in my book *Difficult Behavior in Early Childhood* (Mah, 2007, pp. 69–71). Punishment also assumes that it is normally effective and appropriate. It may be presented in conjunction with rewards, with thoughtful nuances regarding specificity. "Rewarding children for good behavior teaches them more than does punishing them for bad behavior. But sometimes the child's behavior requires correction and just a frown hasn't been enough. Some

> If a tantrum is an expression of the internal emotional process of a child, punishing these natural motivations denies the child's basic human energy.

more impressive kind of punishment is needed" (Granger, 1995, p. 28). Punishment may be effective in stopping a tantrum but not addressing the underlying issue that prompted it in the first place.

Ignore the child (one of the most common recommendations, and closely related to punishment). The premise is that the child is seeking attention inappropriately, giving the attention would reinforce the tantrum, and without the attention and reinforcement, the tantrum will extinguish itself. Unfortunately, an ignored child may become more distraught, despairing, and may intensify to the point of harming self, others, or the environment. Pediatrician Dr. Bill Sears (2006) is something of an exception when he says, "In general, don't ignore a frustration tantrum. Turning away from her behavioral problems deprives her of a valuable support resource, while you lose the chance to improve your rapport with your tantrumer." More experts, however seem to recommend ignoring a tantruming child, including a child who tantrums to get attention. For example, in answering the question, "What's the best way to handle a tantrum?" Dr. Jay L. Hoecker (2006) of the Mayo Clinic states,

> Children have tantrums because they want your attention. It doesn't matter if the attention is positive or negative. . . . So if you lose your cool and yell, or have a tantrum yourself, you've given them what they want. If you can, it's best to pretend to ignore a tantrum. At home, you can act as if it's not interrupting things. After they quiet down, you may be able to negotiate with them, saying, "I noticed your behavior, but that won't get my attention."

Many experts present attention seeking as inherently inappropriate if done through a tantrum. Thus, they recommend ignoring, threatening, or punishing the approach. Although the presentation of a request as a tantrum may need adjustment, the request itself for attention still needs to be honored. Children do not just want adults' attention without an underlying urgency. Getting adults' attention serves to get what they need, whether it is an emotional need such as validation or nurturing, a physical need or desire (toy or candy), or some other childhood urgency. Many times, children do not necessarily want an adult's attention but rather the adult's emotional or physical availability due to some anxiety. Readily accessible adult availability is what allows a child to virtually ignore you right up until the telephone rings. Once you have answered the phone and you become unavailable, availability anxiety ignites. Arbitrary demands, urgencies, and crises suddenly demand your attention—in actuality, the child demands your availability. Hoecker intensifies the anxiety with the additional suggestion to say, "'You're in timeout and, as far as I'm concerned, you're invisible to me.' You pretend that you don't even see the child, but you can still assure his or her safety. Up until the age of 5, magic is real to children. So if you say they're invisible to you, they'll believe it." This recommendation could well stop a tantrum immediately. However, rather than responding to a possible call for help, it threatens a complete emotional annihilation of the child.

> An ignored child may become more distraught, despairing, and may intensify to the point of harming self, others, or the environment.

Distract the child. Distraction (another very common recommendation) purposely draws or directs the child's attention away from whatever is motivating the tantrum to some other thing or issue. It is ironic that distraction is presented as a discipline or guidance method. The term *discipline* comes from the root word of *disciple*. Discipline is training to lead a healthy life. Adults discipline children to help them learn productive beliefs, values, and behaviors as individuals and members in relationships and of communities. Distraction is not discipline! If it teaches anything to the child at all, it teaches that adults disrespect and wish to ignore the child's urgency or need. "I want the ball!" is responded with, "Play with the doll . . . here's something to eat . . . (what you want isn't important to me!)." Under the guise of discipline, numerous experts highly recommend distraction. Journalist and former educator Paul Kropp (2001) points out how seductive distraction can be to adults who are dealing with children's behavior:

> [M]any parents found an easy way out—distraction . . . it's so much easier not to discipline at all. Distraction was the alternative, at least for little kids. If a kid won't eat his green beans, and we don't have the time to encourage, wheedle, whine or demand . . . we put Cool Whip topping on them. Distraction makes the distasteful aspects of growing up more palatable, it seems, and takes the edge off of difficulty. . . . Providing there is something available with which to distract. . . . children can be deflected from going after what they really want by accepting whatever it is we give. . . . (p. 74)

> Distraction is not discipline!

Many experts add a seemingly innocuous caveat to their recommendation to use distraction. "Distraction involves changing the child's focus from an activity that is unacceptable to one that is acceptable without directly confronting the inappropriate behavior. Distraction works very well with children under the age of three" (Albrecht & Miller, 2001, p. 44). Others estimate that the distraction works with tantrums up until about age three or four. After that, I guess you and the children are out of luck! Distractions may stop or derail the tantrum but do nothing to address the underlying issues of the tantrum. No learning or experience with managing disappointment, other feelings or needs, no skills development in problem solving, no balancing self-care with seeking help, no practice articulating needs to others . . . no discipline about living life well. Distraction after 3 or 4 years does not work anymore; because children's needs and urgencies are lifelong human challenges, they eventually become too smart to be distracted. As I tell my child clients, "You can fool me. You can fool me or your parents or teacher for a long time. But you won't fool me forever. And the longer it takes for me to figure out that you've been fooling me or lying to me, the more furious I'm going to be when I find out!" Distraction may not be the best intervention even at young ages. Susan G. O'Leary (1995) states from her research:

> We have also learned that mothers are less effective when they try to distract their misbehaving children than when they use clear reprimands. In fact, when distraction does not work and mothers change their tactics to reprimanding, children become upset, as though they are offended by the change. On the other hand, children are not particularly upset when they are consistently and prudently reprimanded. Distraction may be less effective than reprimanding because distraction provides positive attention to misbehavior. (p. 12)

When a child throws a tantrum, distracting them to something else desirable is rewarding them for tantruming! Distraction, rather than being a discipline for more positive living, becomes encouragement to throw more tantrums. The tantrum may not get them what they wanted originally, but it still gets them something else they discover they want. If you're digging for diamonds and end up with gold, you'll keeping digging your shovel in and throwing dirt over your shoulders! Children who are responded to with distraction will keep digging their heels in and throwing those tantrums. In addition, Reid, O'Leary, and Wolff (1994) state,

> Mothers who initially responded to transgressions with reprimands were later able to use distraction without adverse effects. Conversely, mothers who attempted to manage behavior with distraction first were less effective, and their children transgressed to a great deal. When these mothers did implement the more effective strategy of reprimanding transgressions, their children cried and whined at high rates, behaviors likely to punish their mother's use of better discipline. (p. 244)

In other words, when children were reprimanded after prior distraction attempts (their parents either successfully fooling them or trying to fool them), they became furious for having been fooled! The punishing behavior they described is the intensification of the tantruming behavior. Sometimes, a child or teenager won't get what they want. It may be very disappointing and extremely upsetting. Falling back on the distraction tactic ignores the child or teenager's disappointment and upset. You don't always get your way—reality isn't always fun. Honor the disappointment and upset, and hold the line as the adult. Distracting children from tantrums or other upset may be adults' attempts to avoid responsibility to make difficult discipline choices and engage in difficult processes.

There can be negative consequences, even as some approaches succeed in stopping the tantrum. When adults understand that temper tantrums may have differing underlying causes, adults discover alternative positive discipline versus always using punishment. Better communication; meeting children's needs; and breaking negative patterns and cycles of frustration, anger, negative behavior, and violence result in positive discipline. Discipline becomes more than merely controlling behavior. Parents and other adults often feel extremely frustrated, angry, and ineffective when dealing with a child temper tantrum. The potential for tantrums and even abuse by the adult becomes greater as the adult feels more ineffective over time.

MULTI-ISSUE THEORY OF TANTRUMS

Although the orderly approach for understanding behavior discussed in earlier chapters is useful with tantrum prevention, when a tantrum is full blown, discerning types of tantrums is necessary. Many experts name only two types of tantrums: frustration tantrums and demanding tantrums. Schmitt (2006a) names five types of tantrum, with recommendations for responses to each:

1. Support and help children having frustration- or fatigue-related tantrums.

2. Ignore attention-seeking or demanding-type tantrums.

3. Physically move children having refusal-type or avoidance-type tantrums.

4. Use time-outs for disruptive-type tantrums.

5. Hold children who are having harmful or rage-type tantrums.

Schmitt's five types mix different underlying issues and different expressions. Fatigue can cause frustration, but frustration can come from other issues as well. In fact, frustration, fatigue-related tantrums, demanding-type tantrums, and refusal-type or avoidance-type tantrums, which imply underlying issues, can all be expressed differently. All of them can become disruptive-type tantrums, harmful or rage-type tantrums, or be subtly expressed: sulking, the silent treatment, or passive-aggressive behavior. They can also be expressed with self-destructive behavior, especially as individuals get older, such as gambling, unhealthy relationships, overeating, alcohol, or drugs. Focusing on how tantrums are expressed may not be beneficial because there is an infinite variety of ways in which tantrums are expressed.

Conceptualizing temper tantrums as having four basic underlying issues is helpful. In this book, the four different types of tantrums refer to their four different underlying issues, rather than how they are expressed. Each of the four types of tantrums may be expressed in many different ways. For most tantrums, one of four possibilities is the primary issue in the tantrum. Although there are elements of all four issues in most tantrums, tantrum resolution interventions should be directed at the dominant underlying issue. Each type of tantrum directs a logical intervention response that will be the most effective and efficient in resolving the tantrum.

> Each type of tantrum directs a logical intervention response that will be the most effective and efficient in resolving the tantrum.

The following is a summary of the tantrum types, the primary underlying issues, and the intervention responses.

Correctly recognizing the type of tantrum implies recognizing the primary underlying issue. There is no single magic wand for tantrums, but there are four underlying issues to identify that become the four keys to activating the appropriate intervention. Time to begin unlocking the one-minute temper tantrum solution!

Type of Tantrum	Primary Issue	Response
Manipulative	Power and control	Set boundaries and limits
Upset	Distress	Validation and nurturing
Helpless	Despair	Empowerment
Cathartic	Built-up stress	Permission and guidance to release

CHAPTER HIGHLIGHTS

- Common remedies to temper tantrums have underlying assumptions that may not be correct or appropriate. These remedies include indulging, nurturing, shaming, punishment, ignoring, and distraction.
- Nurturing or indulging a tantruming child assumes that emotional needs expressed must be met. Indulgence implies a greater frailty.
- Ignoring or punishing a tantruming child does not distinguish between a desire or a need for attention that may be appropriate, versus an inappropriate expression to meet that desire or need.
- Distraction ignores and dismisses children's disappointments and does not teach any skills that prevent later tantrums. Using distraction with young children may create more intense tantrums when children are older.
- There are four types of temper tantrums, with four primary underlying issues that lead to four appropriate responses:
  1. Manipulative → power and control → set boundaries and limits
  2. Upset → distress → validation and nurturing
  3. Helpless → despair → empowerment
  4. Cathartic → built-up stress → permission and guidance to release

Manipulative Tantrums

8

Power and Control

"Ahhhhh!" A scream rips through the classroom. It's coming from the back. "No! Stop it!" What is it now? "Ahhhhh! Stop hitting me!" You come from the front of the room. It's Volume 54, no. 12 . . . in the ongoing serial saga, "The Battle of the Cool T-Rex," the epic struggle continues. "It's my turn! You took it last time. I hate you! Teacher! Make her stop!" "Make him stop!" What do I do? Who is right? Who is wrong? Who cares? (Not me!)

They act like having that stupid toy is a life-and-death struggle! Two temper tantrums at the same time. If I let him have the dinosaur, she feels betrayed and gets sullen. If I let her have the dinosaur, he will say he doesn't want to be in my class anymore and throw a bigger fit. If I take away the toy altogether, they both hate me! Is he right? Is she right? Am I going crazy? Are these the joys of teaching!? Ahhhhh! I think King Solomon would have cut the dang T-Rex (or maybe the kids?) in half!

In the above situation, power and control issues have manifested in having or not having the T-Rex. Intuitively, the adults realize that there are power and control issues in many discipline problems. Discipline problems often are management problems adults have with children's attempts to get power and control. Management problems occur when the behavior physically or emotionally disrupts adults or other children. Sometimes it is disruptive to the adult because of the adult's issues with power and control: "Now this little character is messing with my power and control. Who does he/she think he/she is? With my own kids or in my own classroom, I still can't be the boss!?" Children don't consider adults' power and control issues as they exercise lifelong power and control in their lives over the T-Rex!

> From birth, children are actively engaged in constructing their own understandings from their experiences, and these understandings are mediated by and clearly linked to the sociocultural context. Young children actively learn from observing and participating with other children and adults, including parents and teachers. Children need to form their own hypotheses and keep trying them out through social interaction, physical manipulation, and their own thought processes—observing what happens, reflecting on their findings, asking questions, and formulating answers. When objects, events, and other people challenge the working model that the child has mentally constructed, the child is forced to adjust the model or alter the mental structures to account for the new information. (National Association for the Education of Young Children, 2007)

> Discipline problems often are management problems adults have with children's attempts to get power and control.

Adult responses force children to adjust or learn whether tantruming or other behavior fit into their life processes. Adults adjust and struggle throughout their lives for a better education, a good job, or a higher income. Even the struggle for the nonmaterial benefits in life—serenity, fulfillment, security, a sense of purpose, or spirituality—can be seen as gaining power and control in your emotional and psychological life. This happens in relationships as well, including adult relationships. Dr. Meir Wikler (2003), in addressing how to deal with a spouse's anger, advises,

> Present clear alternatives to tirades. One of the main reasons people tend to lose control of their tempers is that they feel helpless, frustrated and wholly ineffective in communicating their feelings. Just as young children will resort to hitting when they are incapable of asserting themselves verbally, so, too, adults will resort to temper tantrums when they feel they are not being heard. And one of the primary reasons they are not getting their needs met is that they have not learned how to express themselves clearly and directly.

Children succeed or fail in pushing for power and control in their lives at home, on the playground, at school . . . at Toys "R" Us. They develop or fail to develop skills for their lifelong struggle for power and control. Without a secure sense of power and control acquired in childhood, battles in later adult relationships of marriage, work, friendships, and acquaintances become problematic. Is the struggle or communication socially responsible? Is communication respectful or contaminated with angry tantrums? Are other people harmed or respected? Are other people's rights ignored? Do other people end up losing their power and control when such children assert theirs? Are children learning that tantrums, however disruptive, work to get their way? Do you get a promotion while your colleagues get stiffed? Do you get to keep playing with the truck while your little brother gets . . . to cry in the corner? Do you honor or betray your ideal self in gaining power and control? Power and control may be acquired, but are healthy values and boundaries also developed?

> Without a secure sense of power and control acquired in childhood, battles in later adult relationships of marriage, work, friendships, and acquaintances become problematic.

STRUGGLES FOR POWER AND CONTROL START EARLY

Sometimes children experience being overcontrolled by their adults. Adults decide what they wear, what they eat, what time to get up and go to sleep, who and what to play with, what they can do with their bodies, what to read, and sometimes even what they are supposed to feel and think. Is it surprising to find them fighting back? A power struggle? Imagine that you are squared off in a boxing match with an itty-bitty kid with humongous boxing gloves. You're in a power struggle with a kid, but worse yet, you're losing! Unresolved issues contaminate adults' acceptance of children's developmentally appropriate struggles for power and control. There's nothing like becoming a parent (or teacher) to bring up all the emotional and psychological garbage that you had thought you had already discarded! Community college child development students were asked to come up with ten qualifications they should meet before becoming a parent. The students, aged 20 to 60, including some who were parents and grandparents themselves, came up with excellent requirements. However, when asked if they had fulfilled these requirements before they became parents, they laughed. Very few said that they had been "qualified" before having children. Most of us learn to parent or teach on the run as an on-the-job training process, helping children deal with power and control issues while still dealing with our own. What if they are abusive or doing dangerous things? Power without sensitivity or control without responsibility is dangerous, within the family or classroom and for individuals. Develop children with self-esteem, with a sense of power and control, who will not become tyrants.

"GOTCHA!! GOTCHA!! GOTCHA!!"

The illusion of power and control becomes compellingly attractive. Passive-aggressive behavior, a type of tantrum, often becomes the major way people gain a sense of power and control. Unfortunately, passive-aggressive behavior does not gain true power and control. Very few people, especially children, just give up and acquiesce to being overpowered and overcontrolled. If unsafe to overtly defy dominating people, children find other ways to gain a sense of power and control. The teacher tries to get a permanent marking pen back from Misty. Misty just can't defy the bigger and meaner adult! So what does she do? In her head, she intuitively thinks,

> *"I have to give it to him. So I give it to him. I will. Yep, I will . . . but I will do it . . . slowly! Slowly. . . . Very slowly. . . . As slowly as I can! If he tells me to hurry up, I say in an outraged self-righteous voice, 'Whaaat?! I'm coming! Can't you wait? What's your hurry?' I delay as much as I can. If he gets upset, all the better—it's working! He threatens me again. Okay okay . . . 'I'm coming. Geez, what's the rush?' I imply with my tone and body language that there is something wrong with him for being so impatient. Finally, still going as slowly as I can get away with, I hold the pen out to him . . . just slightly out of his reach!*

The teacher gets more aggravated. Whoever said patience is a virtue didn't have or work with children! He loses it and yells, "Give it to me now!" He can't believe that he's sounding like that ogre he swore never to be!

> *"Here . . ." Misty says, keeping it slightly out of reach.*

How come she can't just put it in his hand? Why go through all this? "Put it in my hand!" he screams, veins popping in his head.

> *Misty moves the pen slightly closer . . . and just as he is about to grab it . . . she . . . she . . . drops it on the floor! Hah!! Yesss!! Yesss!! Gotcha!! Gotcha!! Gotcha!! Ohhhh! Check out the look on his face! Gotcha!! Gotcha!! Gotcha!! If he says 'Why did you drop it?,' she responds, 'Whaaat? I didn't do nuthin'! You dropped it. I can't help it if you drop it! Geez!'"*

Whether you would call this a tantrum or perhaps acting out, it clearly is an attempt to gain a sense of power and control. Aggravating mom, frustrating dad, annoying the teacher, "misplacing" the paperwork, taking twenty minutes to take your fifteen-minute break, rolling your eyes, gossiping, and mimicking the boss are examples of passive-aggressive behavior. Recognize passive-aggressive behavior as a temper tantrum. The motivation for

> Passive-aggressive behavior, a type of tantrum, often becomes the major way people gain a sense of power and control.

power and control is appropriate, but the technique is dysfunctional. This is learned behavior, after prior overt choices have been intimately involved in the entire process. You may be the frustrating person in the relationship who caused the passive-aggressive behavior or be the target of aggression.

"NO . . . NOPE . . . UH-UH . . . NO WAY! WHAT? . . . THAT'S STUPID!"—IMPACT

What do you want for lunch? How about a peanut butter and jelly sandwich?
 No, I hate peanut butter and jelly sandwiches!

How about a tuna fish sandwich?
 You know I hate tuna fish!

Well, what do you want for lunch?
 I don't know.

How about some soup? (Oh heck, here we go. . . . Again!)
 I don't want soup.

You want me to make some macaroni and cheese?
 I'm sick of macaroni and cheese!

(The pressure is on. Gotta come up with something else, or else!) How about some cheese and crackers?
 No!

(Gotta think . . .) How about some instant noodles?
 MSG is in those things! You trying to kill me!?

(Oh my. Gotta come up with something else . . . gotta come up with something else . . .) how about . . . ? Or . . . ? Maybe. . . . ?
 No . . . Nope . . . Uh-uh . . . no way! What? . . . That's stupid! I hate this! I hate you! But. . . . Make me another offer anyway so I can reject it too!

Children and teenagers may use negativity, another version of passive-aggressive behavior, to manipulate adults. The adult suggests a solution or option to the child. One offer after another, the child rejects each suggestion with mini tantrums. "Please me or else I will reject you. Also, since you can't please me, I reject you." Frantic adults try their hardest to come up with another offer just to be met with angry disdain. By being negative and rejecting every offer, the child keeps control and power over the adult. The child manipulates the adult emotionally back and forth, from hope to despair, from calm to anxiety, and from love to anger and resentment. It's a lousy way to get power and control, but maybe the only way available to some children to get it. They become critical adults, whose negativity or mini tantrums rain on your parade, attack dreams, stomp on optimism, and discourage you from trying. They may claim to be "supportive," "practical," "realistic," or doing it "out of love to keep you from being disappointed."

Adults often hypothesize that the underlying source for a child's acting out is a need for attention. Ironically, adults respond to "Attend to my need for power and control!" by ignoring the child! Ignoring the tantrum may teach what the child shouldn't and cannot do, but it doesn't teach them what to do. Totally ignoring the child also ignores the child's need for power and control. The confirmation that he or she does not count and is not worthy may drive the child either into more severe acting out, intense anger, or depression. It is normal for very young children to have challenges in creating and making constructive impact on the world. Unfortunately, many adults inadvertently ask children to function at higher levels of developmental ability than is realistic. This may be the requirement to figure out how to appropriately gain power and control. Without sufficient guidance, children experiment with a behavior (passive-aggressive behavior, negativity, or a tantrum), experience failure, and are ignored. Still without guidance, they try something else creative that adults deem unacceptable or throw a tantrum. Failing again and punished or ignored again, a subsequent temper tantrum may be a protest against the expectation for performance beyond one's social-emotional capacity. Passive-aggressive behavior may be their creative way to make you pay attention. And it works! So there!

> Ignoring the tantrum may teach what the child shouldn't and cannot do, but it doesn't teach them what to do.

CONSEQUENCES IN POWER AND CONTROL—"THAT'S NOT FAIR!"

> *Can I have it? Please . . . please . . . pretty please. . . . I won't ask for anything else. I'll be good. Please, I won't ask for anything later. Please . . . Okay, I'll get for you.*

Thank you thank you thank you

(Okay. I set the limits, I offered the choices, and I made clear the consequences).

On to next week. *Ooooh! It's so neat! Kim has one. I want it. Buy it for me . . .*

No. I spent all that money last week at the fair.

But I want one! I need one! **Everyone** *has one! I'll be good. Please . . . please . . . pretty please. . . . Please. I have to have one. Please, I'll be good. . . . No!? Kim's mom always buys her stuff. That's not fair! Please!? I'll be the* **only** *kid who doesn't have one. . . .* **I HATE you! I hate you!** *You* **never** *get me anything! You* **always** *get things for Johnny! That's not fair! You like Johnny better!* **I hate you! I hate you!** *. . .*

(Oh no! Here they come . . . tears, sulking, the silent treatment, screaming, tantrums . . . a multitude of possible combinations to punish me. My baby hates me! Oh, the pain! I'm so mean. . . . My baby hates me! People are looking at me . . . how embarrassing! It's just money. What is the big deal?) Well . . . just this time.

Thank you! Thank you! You're the best mommy ever! Thank you thank you thank you! I won't ask you for anything else ever. I don't care about anything else. Thank you thank you thank you!

As you enjoy the glow of appreciation and relish in a child's joy, a little voice says, "Won't be sorry, huh? Yeah, right! How come you feel that you just sold your soul?" And that there will be many times you will pay the price. The kid made a bad choice spending money, being passive-aggressive, being negative, or tantruming, and you just made a worse one by indulging the kid. Another potential poor choice by adults is to manipulate children to make the right decisions. Teachers or parents may encourage, guide toward, reason, intimidate, or threaten children to make the proper choice. Any other than the adult's recommended choice becomes the wrong choice.

"Pick whatever you want. Oh. Are you sure that's what you want? Isn't this one nice too? I don't think that was as nice. What do you think? Well. Are you sure? I really like this one. So, that's the one you want? Uh huh. . . . Well, let's think about it for a while. We'll come back."

Adults implicitly threaten displeasure with children, who quickly figure out pleasing them is safer. Overtly, the child hears that he or she has power but never feels in control. Coerced to deny themselves, they become confused about their reality. Eventually, they realize making the right choices doesn't serve them. Tantrums, defiance, and disruption may result. Children need to experience real choices and the consequences of those choices. People often learn the most from making poor choices and suffering the negative consequences. Some poor choices are too harmful and must be prevented. However, a wise person learns from the mistakes of others; the average person learns from his or her own; and the fool does not learn despite continued mistakes. The wisdom that we give to children usually comes from our mistakes, made while ignoring others' wisdom! Parents might warn their children not to spend all their money and save some for later. However, adults should avoid making threats. Threats are manipulations to force a child do something he or she doesn't want. Name the consequences that may result. Threats intimidate, whereas setting and asserting consequences teaches about life processes. Despite clear consequences, most young children focus on the present and choose what is exciting right now. Later they would be so broke, so sad, so pathetic, and so whiny when they discover that the exciting choice has negative consequences! Many parents cannot endure their sadness, which is a negative consequence, and buy the new toy. Adults might say, "Didn't I tell you?" and otherwise threaten or admonish (blah blah blah blah). However, they have rewarded the negative choice with a positive consequence. The solution to the manipulative tantrum is based on these clear principles:

- Children seek power and control, but may do so inappropriately, including tantruming.
- Setting a boundary is the first step. Boundaries come before the possibility of growth and change.
- You must also assert and defend the boundary.
- Consequences reinforce the boundaries.
- Boundaries and consequences promote responsibility, which is appropriate power and control.

When a child throws a temper tantrum that is essentially manipulative and about power and control, the response needs to be of setting boundaries. In setting the boundaries, you allow for a positive resolution to gain power and control without allowing negative habits to develop. The response is not just only about stopping a manipulative tantrum but also about helping the child meet his or her needs for power and control in socially acceptable and individually healthy ways.

> In setting the boundaries, you allow for a positive resolution to gain power and control without allowing negative habits to develop.

"OK. No one is going to have the T-Rex toy if you keep yelling and fighting. If you keep fighting, I'm going to put the toy away for the next week.

I don't care who had it last. I only care that you are fighting. If I have to decide who should get the toy, I decide that no one gets it. If you want it, you two decide how to take turns or to play with it together.

If you cannot do that, then I will put it away. I do not need to have the T-Rex toy in the classroom. I need you two to stop fighting and screaming. Understand?

I'm taking it. You have two minutes to come up with a plan for sharing. Or I will put it away.

Note that the teacher doesn't shame, ignore, distract, indulge, or punish the kids. The kids may choose a consequence that is punishing to them, if they choose not to negotiate a solution. The teacher didn't have to decide who gets the toy or what is fair. The teacher decides what is acceptable or unacceptable. It is acceptable to want to have the T-Rex. It is not acceptable to be violent and disruptive in wanting it. The teacher has accepted that there might be two upset T-Rex-less kids soon. Boundaries are given and consequences are delineated. If the children decide to be reasonable and negotiate a way to play with the toy, then the consequence is they get to play with it. They have to come up with a solution, not the teacher. They already made a negative choice by fighting or tantruming. If they make another negative choice by not coming up with a solution, then the consequence is that they do not get to play with it for a week. They have tantrumed to gain more power and control and tried to manipulate the teacher to decide in each of their respective favors. The teacher's response teaches that they cannot get power and control this way, but their desire for power and control is honored. They are led, guided, and taught to gain it by being reasonable and negotiating with each other. If they can't be reasonable, the consequence is the loss of power and control to have that wonderful T-Rex toy! The T-Rex toy becomes a social-emotional teaching opportunity instead of a stupid toy to fight over! A one-minute temper tantrum solution!

CHAPTER HIGHLIGHTS

- How well adults set limits and guide children in appropriately seeking power and control in their lives creates childhood consequences and eventually lifelong consequences.

- Children who do not get appropriate power and control in their lives may resort to passive-aggressive behavior and negativity to gain the illusion of power and control.
- Ignoring a manipulative tantrum ignores the child's need for power and control and may drive the child into more severe acting out, intense anger, or depression.
- Adults need to apply not only positive consequences to children when they make positive choices but also negative consequences when they make negative choices.
- An effective response to a manipulative tantrum is to set boundaries that allow for a positive resolution to gain power and control without allowing negative habits to develop.

Upset Temper Tantrums

9

Distress

UPSET TANTRUMS—VALIDATION

I can hear the screaming and crying from my office. It has been going on for a couple of minutes. I can hear Mickey screaming, "It's my turn!" and the teacher screaming back, "No, it's not! Didn't I already tell you? You can't run this group! You stop it!"

Here they come again! The teacher stomps into my office, with Mickey in tow. Angrily, she puts him on the couch, "He's got to learn he can't just have his way all the time! I don't have time to deal with his fighting me!" She stomps off to rejoin her group of three-year-old kids, which is now (of course) in chaos.

Tears are streaming down Mickey's face; his face is red; his entire body shakes with the hiccups. I turn my chair toward him . . . less than a minute later, he has calmed down, acknowledged what he needs to do to be with his group, and is going off to rejoin his group where he is able to cooperate again. Why? What happened?

The child had lost it. The teacher had lost it. And now it was in my lap as the director. The teacher got caught up in the drama and gotten ignited. She had interpreted Mickey's behavior as a power struggle that she was losing. His three-year-old child tantrum had caused her twenty-seven-year-old adult tantrum. Mickey's tantrum was an upset tantrum, not a manipulative tantrum. Treating it as if it were a power and control issue and "not letting him get away with it!" had made it worse. This teacher's power and control issues were easily ignited when children were challenging. Individuals who have control issues have made a serious career error in choosing to be teachers! As an upset tantrum, the underlying issue was of distress. Adults need to evaluate the feelings involved and not reject the feelings implicitly by judging the circumstances. To Mickey, the circumstances justify his feelings, regardless if anyone else in the world agrees. He is instantly in distress! His tantrum was not a choice made dispassionately or logically to control the teacher. Carolyn Chambers Clark (2007) comments on the temperamental tantrum that is applicable to Mickey:

> With the temperamental tantrum, the child is not very adaptable and is suddenly asked to do something and she can't adjust quickly enough. If you look at your reaction neutrally, you will find you feel sorrier for your child in this case. You believe, "she can't help it." Realize the child probably can't help it. Put yourself in his shoes and see if you wouldn't feel out frustrated, angry and out of control, too. Be sympathetic. If you decide it's a temperamental tantrum, be kind and sympathetic. Take the attitude, I know this is tough for you and I'll help you to bring this to an end. (Clark, 2007)

The teacher did not have the compassion to understand why or even realize that Mickey was in distress. He was just unreasonable! Mickey was too young to control emotions that burst forth and too young to stop and articulate his feelings to the teacher. Not that she wanted to hear it!

> Adults need to evaluate the feelings involved and not reject the feelings implicitly by judging the circumstances.

The tantrum started with Mickey getting upset, crying, and grabbing a toy. Mickey's teacher interpreted Mickey's disruptive behavior as an attack on her control of the classroom. Mickey's reaction was of defense and anger at not getting the toy, being dismissed, and being raged at by the teacher. Since the teacher could not resist her instinct to interpret negatively, the battle proceeded. Of course, Mickey and Mickey's teacher preferred that nothing happen negatively in the first place. Don't we all! Everyone prefers that others adjust and modulate their behavior. Mickey's teacher just wanted him to be good. Adding complexity, distress for Mickey, who is a temperamentally difficult child, is more challenging than for many other children. Thomas, Chess, and Birch (1970) remind us, "In general our studies indicate that a demand that conflicts excessively with any temperamental characteristics and capacities is likely to place a child under heavy and even unbearable stress. This means that parents and teachers need to recognize what a specific child can and cannot do . . ." (¶ 19). Mickey could not react any differently. His temperamental traits included low sensory threshold and low adaptability. He was highly stimulated in preschool to the edge of overwhelm and had rigid responses so that he could not adapt when they failed. He could not wait readily without getting upset. For Mickey, delayed gratification was very difficult and consequences—whether positive or negative—were hard for him to understand. Prior experience was forgotten or irrelevant to the moment. The teacher had already told him that he needed to wait. She had already told him that everyone has to take turns, both this time and many times before. How many times had the teacher been told that young kids, especially impulsive three-year-old kids, don't remember when excited in the moment!? Imagine that . . . a three year old acting like a three year old. And imagine that . . . a twenty-seven year old acting like a three year old.

Address and honor the distress and the interpretation of its cause. "Oh, you thought you weren't going to get a turn. You'll get a turn. It didn't feel fair not to get a turn, wasn't it? I'm sorry you have to wait. It's hard to wait. It'll be OK, you'll get it next." This is fundamentally different from, "Stop making a fuss. It's not your turn. It's Jane's turn. You have to wait. You don't have to get so upset." Mickey did have to get upset . . . it's who and what he is! In both sets of responses, the misinterpretation is noted and corrected, but only in the first response is the child's distress noted and honored. Barb Grady (2007), counselor and child development instructor, states,

> Children can do one of three things with these feelings: express them, repress them, or release them. Holding feelings inside (repression) is not mentally or physically healthy. It is important that children (and adults) have opportunities and methods for expressing their feelings. . . . Adults in our culture often deny their feelings and may lead children to hold their feelings in check. . . . A tantrum is like an emotional sneeze. . . . It doesn't help children when their misbehavior is ignored or when reasonable limits aren't set. Children rely on us to let them know what is OK and what is not OK. Step in when your child is going off track and gently but firmly prevent any hurting, grabbing, throwing, destruction, withdrawal, or giving up. Go ahead and limit the child, physically stopping the behavior, but allow the feelings while you are holding those limits. Tantrums, crying, trembling, and perspiring in the release of fear, and all the loud noises that go along with that release, are not misbehavior. They are part of a healing process.

Mickey's tantrum seemed much more than an emotional sneeze, but, like a sneeze, it could not be held back. Boundaries needed to be set, but in the second response, the distress is noted and rejected as illogical or uncalled for. Mickey became wrong for having had distress. Instead of drawing any nurturing from the teacher, Mickey drew anger and scorn. When an adult honors the child's distress, he or she is not automatically confirming the child's incorrect interpretation of reality. Interpretations come from prior experiences and inexperience, healthy and unhealthy learning, religious guidelines, and family and cultural orientations. This was as true for the teacher as it was for Mickey. Unfortunately, some people's egocentrism or stress responses preclude any interpretation other than their own when a child is in distress, tantruming, or acting out. Without nurturing, the child will continue until finally getting the connection or validation, or until completely depleted. Whether the child was right or wrong does not deny the necessity of making the connection or validating the feeling of distress. No matter how a teacher, parent, or anyone else evaluates the logic or appropriateness of the reaction, action, or feelings of distress, the sense of pain, abuse, and terribly unfair treatment is absolutely real to the child! Unfortunately for Mickey, his teacher could not accept Mickey's emotional distress as valid.

> No matter how a teacher, parent, or anyone else evaluates the logic or appropriateness of the reaction, action, or feelings of distress, the sense of pain, abuse, and terribly unfair treatment is absolutely real to the child!

HOW TO CONNECT AND VALIDATE

The four basic ways to validate a child in distress, even when in an exploding upset tantrum, are the following:

- touch
- facial expression and body language
- voice tone
- a validating message

When these four validations are applied, then the child is usually much more able to integrate the messages that follow.

Touch. This would be any kind of gentle physical connection: a hand on the shoulder or back, holding hands, putting an arm around shoulder, putting the child on the adult's lap. This is a warm cuddling touch, not an angry touch; an encompassing touch, not a restraining touch. Touch works better with tantrum throwers who have motor-kinesthetic learning styles than visual or auditory approaches. With a kind and gentle touch, your facial expression, body language, and voice tone tend to automatically modulate to a more nurturing presentation. The old folk remedy of giving the child or person hug when they are having a tantrum comes from touch being an incredibly powerful validating force.

Something had happened, and it was obvious that Tsuneo was unhappy. When his mom asked what was going on, his response was, "You'll get mad at me if I tell you." She was consumed with fears about all kinds of horrible things. Told to put her four-year-old son in her lap, everything changed. The physical contact immediately gave Tsuneo reassurance of mom's care and nurturing. Tsuneo felt reassured and gained confidence enough to

> Touch works better with tantrum throwers who have motor-kinesthetic learning styles than visual or auditory approaches.

tell her what he was previously afraid she would be upset about. Although many people may have difficulty verbally expressing intimacy and caring, physical instincts prevail to facilitate communication.

Facial expression and body language. Visual connections can be beneficial or harmful. Standing over the child and looking down establishes a superior-to-inferior relationship not compatible with nurturing. Hands on the hip, leaning forward, jaw stuck out, and waving a finger in the face asserts superior hierarchal separation rather than empathetic equality. The child knows immediately that the adult is not connected to his or her distress. Face to face at the child's level creates greater connection and intimacy. An open, gentle face and the relaxed body posture as you bend down shows connection, empathy, and receptive availability. This emphasizes emotional and psychological compassion rather

> An open, gentle face and the relaxed body posture as you bend down shows connection, empathy, and receptive availability.

than adult superiority by virtue of size. Resolution will be through emotional connection. Unfortunately, some adults purposely avoid nurturing nonverbal messages to assert the superior position. Domination is how they intend to force change of behavior.

Voice tone. Auditory communication to the upset child should be soothing and empathetic, embracing, and nurturing. Caring is communicated through a positive and gentle rather than an angry tone. Children can sense adult frustration. When adult frustration turns into anger, especially intense anger, the focus and urgency of children often turn to avoiding or eliminating the anger. Connection is not experienced. Whatever discipline or lesson to be learned is forgotten in the child's urgency to flee or avoid the anger. Simultaneously dealing with his or her own distress and the adult's anger, the child feels even more out of control. Scared or even more distressed, the child may slide into a more severe form of tantruming, the helpless tantrum. A calm voice communicates that the situation is under control although the child has gotten out of control with the tantrum.

All three of the first validations are nonverbal communications. When there is a discrepancy between the verbal and the nonverbal components of communication, instinct assumes that the verbal component is dishonest while the nonverbal component is truthful. If touch, facial expression and body language, and tone are sincere, even clumsy verbal communication will be experienced as sincere. If speech is ostensibly appropriate but the internal emotional or cognitive state is contrary, the nonverbal messages will reveal the insincerity of the communication. Any mismatch between the verbal and nonverbal parts of the communication creates anxiety for the recipient. The words may be reasonable or conciliatory, but the eyes, face, tone, and body tension convey anger. Children hear and understand the words while the nonverbal communication indicates that the words are lies. This increases children's stress rather than relieving it.

Validating message. Verbalized cognitive connection to or labeling upset, distress, or feeling is nurturing: "You're really sad, aren't you?" or "This must really be scary." Verbal communication solidifies the nonverbal communications if it gives the same message. However, verbal communication is often the secondary rather than the primary communication or connection. Verbal solidification is often unnecessary if the physical, visual, and tonal contact is clear. In the movie *Three Men and a Baby* (Cort, 1987), three bachelors raise a baby left on their doorstep. Actor Tom Selleck reads a report of a violent boxing match to the baby Mary, using gentle tones. Steve Gutenberg complains about the brutal imagery upsetting Mary, but Selleck responds that the words don't matter, since the baby doesn't understand anyway. It's only the tone that matters, he asserts. In the television show *Kids Say the Darndest Things*, Bill Cosby often says outrageous and seemingly aggressive things to little children but with obvious humor and gentleness conveyed in face, body, and voice tone. The children giggle delightedly at the funny man playing with them. Sometimes, individuals misinterpret banter between individuals from a nonmainstream community as challenging, disrespectful, or even threatening. "Yo, dog, yo' mama's so stupid that . . . !" However, nonverbal messages simultaneously conveying playfulness and affection mitigate the disrespect to others who are culturally in tune. Written communication, including instant messaging and e-mail communication, lack all the nonverbal cues that clarify intention and meaning. Problems can easily arise due to misinterpretations as people fill in the blanks.

The validating message has no intrinsic approval or disapproval of motivations that cause the feelings that are labeled. The individual's intellectual process that leads to the feelings may be completely erroneous. There was enough for everyone, although the child feared that he or she wouldn't get one. Despite the child's interpretation of events, he or she was not forgotten. People do care about the child. A validating message doesn't address the child's interpretive errors. If your immediate verbal message addresses any misinterpretation or misunderstanding, it has the unfortunate implicit effect of denying the distress. Commentary on the facts without attending to feelings invalidate children. The facts don't count in this moment. Since only the feelings count (right now), naming the feelings becomes validating. "You feel mad, don't you?" or "That's very sad," does not imply that having any feelings are wrong. The validating message is essentially of compassion. Any commentary on the behavior, thought process, or perceptions should be saved. An accusatory or negative tone, moreover, implies that the child should not feel that way, which increases the distress. When validated, individuals may still be sad or have residual upset. However, sadness is a less disruptive and more tolerable state than distress. Handling disappointment or sadness is a necessary part of mental health. Children need more than caring words. They need to experience that caring adults will nurture them when they are distressed and that they do not need to be sad alone.

The socialization message. The second response or lesson, which comes after the validating message, helps children face reality by presenting limits. Socialization teaches a child how to manage and express his or her emotional process and other needs within the boundaries of a community of peers and others. Jumping to the socialization message ignores the child's emotional urgency or distress. Without validation and connection, the child experiences all the socialization lessons and boundaries as dismissive. This can lead to continual self-doubt and low self-esteem. When adults act out, they are often like children seeking a little validation and nurturing. Boundary setting or suggestions fall on deaf ears (both for the child and the adult) if individuals don't feel validated.

I turn my chair toward Mickey. . . . I gesture for him to come to me. Sniffing and sad, Mickey comes to me and leans against my leg; I place my left arm around his shoulders gently and with my right hand I rub his chest and stomach (where tension is held) . . . (gentle nurturing touch) I lean my head down towards his, keeping a gentle expression on my face . . . (empathetic body posture and facial expression) In a quiet compassionate voice, I begin speaking to him . . . (caring tone) I say, "It must be sad for you to get into trouble with the teacher, isn't it? You feel bad don't you?" (I don't repeat rules or make judgments about the circumstances; I speak to his state of being- his feelings) . . . (validating message). Mickey's distress melts; his body relaxes; and he says, "Yeeesss!" in a sad but not angry or distressed voice. Mickey has been heard by someone- he has been validated. Now he feels safe again. NOW, I can tell him and he can hear what he can and cannot do, and what he must do (the socialization message), "Mickey, you need to try to cooperate with the teacher. Okay? Can you go back and tell the teacher you want to try again?" Mickey nods his agreement and trots off back to his group. Less than one minute's elapsed time—a one-minute temper tantrum solution!

The footnote to Mickey's story is that there were many unfruitful attempts to train the teacher. She was unable to accept her role in the mutual temper tantruming. She was unable to work effectively with Mickey. Brazelton and Sparrows' (2005) caution for adults to understand children's anger was more relevant to her than to Mickey: "When a child seems angry most of the time, when his reactions are out of proportion to the causes of his anger, and when his anger interferes with family, friends, and important activities at school, then his anger may be a symptom of a more serious underlying problem . . . a child is also likely to be angry more often, and out of proportion to any immediate trigger" (p. 75) Emotional upset in children may be transitory, or it may be deeper as discussed earlier in examining systemic factors that ignite tantrums. Although this was not the case with Mickey, it was probably the case with the teacher; she was unable or unwilling to address the underlying problems that caused her anger. For all our compassion for her, the program's mission was to serve children, not to facilitate her therapeutic process. She was in the program to serve our mission of serving children. Instead, she desperately protected her own self-esteem and responded with the only solution left to her: the eighth assessment; she morally condemned Mickey as being a bad kid. Angrily self-righteous, she continued her temper tantruming. This was unacceptable, and as a result, she was eventually terminated.

CHAPTER HIGHLIGHTS

- Distress is the underlying energy of an upset tantrum.
- An incorrect or negative interpretation of an upset tantrum leads to invalidating responses that exacerbate the tantrum.
- Validation helps an upset tantrum. Validation can be by touch, facial expression and body language, voice tone, and a validating message. The verbalized validating message is often the less important part of the communication.
- A socialization message can be added after the validation has calmed the child.
- Adults need to accept and address any personal issues that make it difficult for them to assess and respond appropriately to challenging children.

Helpless Temper Tantrums　10

Not Distress but Despair

HELPLESS TANTRUMS—EMPOWERMENT

"It's not fair!! I never get to go first in games. Sheila always gets to go first. Ahhhhhh! No, no, no, no, no! I didn't get to choose. She always gets what she wants. You never listen to me! You hate me! You're mean!"

Adults are often perplexed with the pervasive sense of helplessness in some individuals who seem to have so much positive support and good things going for them. They have caring, attentive parents who seem to indulge these children. Indulgence does not spoil them as with Veruca Salt, who was spoiled by her rich father (Veruca Salt is a character from *Charlie and the Chocolate Factory*, a book by Roald Dahl (1964), and also a movie (Burton, 2005) starring Johnny Depp as Willie Wonka). Veruca Salt's father indulged her every whim when she threw manipulative tantrums. When Veruca announces that she must have a Golden Ticket, the entry to Willy Wonka's magical candy factory, her father buys thousands of Wonka Bars and makes his factory workers open them for her. Veruca has temper tantrums if she doesn't get what she wishes for, and her parents rush to give in to her desire. Instead of being spoiled, some children lose their fundamental sense of safety in the world when parents consistently indulge them. The children subsequently throw helpless tantrums that are an expression of underlying despair. Although helpless tantrums may look like upset tantrums full of distress, they have a deeper and more desperate emotional quality. Children are terrified during a helpless tantrum, and nurturing is never enough to stop the fear. The help-less, despairing child continues to ask for more, as if nurturing had not occurred or was not enough. Misdiagnosis of the tantrum as distress- instead of despair-based leads adults to inadvertently confirm the child's helpless victim stance. The child, through the tantrum, asserts helplessness, despair, and fear. The nurturing adult is inadvertently saying, "Yes, you're correct. You're lucky this time because I will save you!" The continuing cycle of tantrums followed by adult nurturing proves to the child that he or she is and will always be helpless. The helpless tantrum is also unlike Veruca Salt's manipulative tantrum in which the need for power and con-trol is transitory and specific to the circumstances. Instead of fear and despair, Veruca Salt is full of rage. With the helpless tantrum, getting what one wants or one's way does not address the underlying sense of victim-ization or helplessness. Previous positive experiences are forgotten as soon as there is another frustration or failure. Any negative experience symbol-izes the individual's fundamental vulnerability in an uncaring and hostile world. Despite adult nurturing or indulgence of the child's demands, despair continues. The child believes that nothing makes any difference. Continued attempts at nurturing tend to exacerbate the tantrum. Doing well or getting what they want is primarily about luck, and they only have bad luck.

> The adult requires and guides—even forces—the child to assert himself or herself in a powerful and nonhelpless manner.

Adults need to deviate from this fruitless cycle by empowering children. Empowering the child counters the basic assertion of helplessness. The adult requires and guides—even forces—the child to assert himself or herself in a powerful and nonhelpless man-ner. The adult can offer direction, but the child must take the action. The child must be the one asserting power.

A child's sense of surviveability comes from successfully handling the challenges of life, which is developed by trusting adults to be available in such situations. However, getting used to and continuing to depend on being rescued becomes dangerous. Without the ability to independently care for oneself, some individuals develop a helpless personality. Hara Estroff Marano (1995), in an article on bullies and victims in *Psychology Today*, noted that about 22 percent of children experienced being bullied sometime during the school year. However, only 8 to 9 percent of kids became the constant targets of bullies throughout the school year. More than half of the bullied children stopped being the targets of victimiza-tion. Why did that 8 to 9 percent of children become the bullies' favored prey over and over? The helpless or victim personalities' passive rather than assertive approach to conflict may be the reason. They tend not to negotiate with others or persuade them, and they make few or no demands, requests, or even suggestions. Basically, they hope that things will get better ("please please please please please . . . come on, lucky lucky lucky . . . please!"). Unfortunately, since they don't "make their luck," their reality often continues to be miserable. They rarely initiate interactions and tend to be passive in their play. Even as they mature beyond developmentally appropriate parallel play (three years and under), they continue to play next to people rather than with them. They are socially incompetent, not as negative aggressive antisocial people, but because of their inability to negotiate social situations. They seldom have aggressive behavior problems in playgroups, family, or school. However, they cannot handle aggression toward them, which mean they always need to be rescued. They end up feeling worse and more anxious. They are recognized as vulnerable, which leads to targeting by opportunistic and aggressive children. Caring people, including peers and teachers, are initially drawn to care for and help them. However, eventually the same people become frustrating and negative to caregivers as well. For some, it is the whining tantrums that are so off-putting. For others, it is the defeated and depressed energy and attitudes that are so unappealing. Caring for and identifying with a helpless person brings pain to people that care for them. A caring person's own sense of impotence is activated, as they feel helpless just like a victim. The helpless individual never seems able to integrate this help, guidance, and love into their personalities and behavior to become more able and successful. As a result, caring people—even parents—often become angry and dismissive of the helpless child. Then caring people feel guilty rejecting the victim.

> The helpless individual never seems able to integrate this help, guidance, and love into their personalities and behavior to become more able and successful.

HOW HELPLESSNESS IS CREATED

Mommy and baby are going to the park. I love taking baby to the park. The sun . . . the grass . . . the sand . . . with babies at Tot Land. An oasis in the urban desert for baby and me. No dishes, no bills, no news about this or that atrocity somewhere in the world . . . or in New York, Los Angeles . . . or over there . . .

Anything you need . . . anything you'll ever need . . . I'll be there for you honey. Mommy will take care of you, baby. Mommy will take care of you in the big bad ugly world. But . . . we don't have to worry about that, do we? We're in Tot Land! Sunshine, grass, sand, swing, and other sweet babies. . . . Just sweet babies. Right? Just beautiful, sweet babies . . .

Although the helpless personality tends to be sensitive, nonviolent, and nonaggressive, all the children and people with these traits do not become victims. What differentiates positive personal traits for healthy social relationships from vulnerability to becoming helpless? Good intentions of protective and anxious parents and other adults go awry. In protecting children from the real world, these adults actually prevent children from developing the skills to handle aggression and conflict.

> In protecting children from the real world, these adults actually prevent children from developing the skills to handle aggression and conflict.

Little Jordan, 18 months old, is in the sandbox at the Tot Land playground. Mommy has brought him and his little red bucket and little blue shovel to play. The sand feels warm and flows through his fingers. It's fun.

Little Darlene, 20 months old, toddles over to Jordan. They look at each other. Jordan doesn't know Darlene. Is she okay? He looks at his mom. Mom smiles and says, "Say hi to the little girl, Jordan." Mom starts talking to another lady. Jordan stares at Darlene. He doesn't know what to do. Is it okay?

Darlene looks at Jordan. She looks at his bucket. She looks at Jordan. Jordan just watches Darlene. Darlene looks at Jordan. Looks at his bucket and looks at Jordan. She reaches over and grabs his bucket! He holds it tighter, his eyes getting big. Darlene pulls harder. Tears fill Jordan's eyes. Darlene frowns and smiles at the same time. Jordan is getting scared. Darlene gives a big yank. Jordan gets pulled face down into the sand. Darlene has the bucket! Nobody at home snatches things from him! Darlene has the bucket but she's still there watching him. She has a small smile on her face. It's not a pretty or nice smile. It's a scary smile!

His lips begin to quiver. Jordan becoming afraid, looks around. There's his mom. The predator has struck. Wahhh!! Wahhhh!! Waaahhhhhhh!! "I've been violated! Help me! I need help! I can't do it myself!"

Not a manipulative tantrum, although there has been a loss of power and control. Much more than an upset tantrum; it's despair, not distress. Many would consider this an appropriate reaction rather than a tantrum.

Calling it a tantrum seems inappropriate to some, because of the assumption that all tantrums are about manipulation, when in fact this reaction is not about manipulation; rather, this is a helpless tantrum.

Jordan has stepped outside his safe, nurturing, loving world. Darlene doesn't love him and won't do anything for him like Mommy or like Granny. Darlene just took his bucket, and Jordan doesn't know what to do. This is the one of many crises in the real world that will shape Jordan's ability to deal with intrusion, aggression, bullying, or abuse. Jordan's mother turns suddenly at the sound of his desperate cry. Quickly she realizes that some bully girl has attacked! Immediately, she springs into action. There are three paths that she might consider: first, protect little Jordan from the bully; second, let little Jordan handle it by himself; or third, empower and train little Jordan how to deal with bullies. The danger is that she may choose to protect Jordan as if he were truly frail. Having a bucket snatched away is not necessarily destructive of his emotional and psychological being. If Jordan was that vulnerable, she would rush in, take the bucket away from Darlene, and give it back to Jordan. "Here Jordan, poor sad baby. That mean little girl took your bucket. I got it back for you. Mommy made it okay for you." What's wrong with this response? By intervening and resolving the conflict, Jordan learns that Mommy will rescue him. His skills, resources, and resiliency are deemed insufficient for him to take care of himself. His control in the situation came from crying, getting his mother's attention, and getting her to rescue him. He had no direct control or power. His mother's action is a formative nonverbal communication. Rescuing Jordan tells him, "You're not okay," that he cannot handle the situation on his own, and is vulnerable to harm.

THE LOVING THIEF AND A
SELF-FULFILLING PROPHECY

The message becomes a self-fulfilling prophecy. Mommy (or other adult) becomes the loving thief. Mommy not only gave the message that Jordan is incapable and vulnerable, but also stole from him opportunities to learn how to handle conflict and develop resiliency. Jordan becomes ever more incapable because he never gets to practice skills necessary to handle conflict on his own. His fear intensifies as he realizes that Mommy must rescue him or he will suffer—and that Mommy may not always be available to save him. He becomes more likely to throw helpless tantrums when facing challenges. His increased anxiety makes him easily identifiable and thus more vulnerable to predators looking for easy prey. Parents and teachers must decide whether children need to be protected. Protection is compelled when circumstances are overwhelming and/or too dangerous to be handled alone. However, children are often capable of taking care of themselves. Other times, it is difficult or impossible for children to deal with a situation or individual. They will be greatly challenged to succeed or to try and still fail. When adults step in immediately, they steal children's opportunities to struggle successfully; or to perhaps fail in the struggle but find that they can survive the disappointment, loss, or hurt resulting from the failure.

His increased anxiety makes him easily identifiable and thus more vulnerable to predators looking for easy prey.

Children need encouragement, training, and empowerment. Adults can do this only by letting go. Children must struggle and suffer to build necessary skills and resiliency to handle stress; conflicts; and intrusive, abusive, or exploitative people.

> *Jordan, that little girl took your bucket. You don't look happy. Is that okay? No? Take it back. Little girl, Jordan wants to talk to you. Don't go away. Jordan, get your bucket. Get your bucket . . . Mommy won't get it for you. You need to get it. She'll give it back to you.*

(A firm glance at her would be useful here!)

> *Tell her, "No."*

(If Jordan can successfully take it from here, let him do it. If he can't, then ask)

> *You need help? Here she is. Put your hand on the bucket. Hold on.*

(If Jordan can successfully take it from here, let him do it. If he can't, then ask)

> *Okay? Now pull it away.*

(If necessary, close your hand around his hand on the bucket)

> *There you go! You did it! Good job, you got your bucket. What do you want to do with your bucket now? You want to put sand in it? You want to let her play with it? Or play together with her? You decide.*

Empowerment, empowerment, empowerment. Empowerment is a key to developing self-esteem and the key to addressing helpless tantrums.

Competency cannot be acquired without the opportunity to learn. Grit your teeth and clench your fists! Giving children the opportunity to learn largely depends on you handling your own fears for children. As they become competent at meeting challenges and at helping themselves, help-less tantrums become unnecessary. Adults can empower children by iden-tifying the situation, validating their feelings, and suggesting options:

> *Sometimes it's not fair or feels fair. You do get to go first sometimes. Sheila gets to go first sometimes. If you want to go first, or get to choose, or get what you want, this is what you need to do . . . _____ .*

> *Not that. Not screaming and crying. If you want me to listen to you, this is how you talk to me . . .*

> *This is what you say . . . _____ ,*

> *This is what you do . . . _____ . Not that. Not whining and calling me "mean."*

> *If you want help, this is what you need to do . . . _____ .*

> *If you choose not to do these things, then you won't get what you want. Do you want to complain and cry and do the same things that don't work? Or can you do things differently to get more of what you want? You can get what you want."*

Another one-minute temper tantrum solution!

THE GALLANT KNIGHT, THE DAMSEL-IN-DISTRESS, AND THE DRAGON

There is another way that people may do too much for a person with a problem. Many people have life experiences that prompt them to the role of the rescuer or the Gallant Knight, a version of the Hero. Self-definition as the Gallant Knight requires that someone else accept the role of either the Damsel-in-Distress or some fire-breathing Dragon. You become the Dragon to slay if you get into conflict with the Gallant Knight. Any prob-lem becomes a mission or crusade for the Gallant Knight to conquer. Any person with a problem becomes the Damsel-in-Distress, offering opportu-nity for fulfillment to the Gallant Knight. This dynamic is often manifested in a stereotypical interchange between men and women. "I have a problem at work," says she. Immediately, he comes out in his superhero Problem-Solving-Man costume. Ta-daaah! "I can fix that! Why don't you do this? Why don't you do that?" This sets off a cycle of unsuccessful communications. She says, "No, that's not it. You don't understand." He offers, "Why don't you do this? Or do that?" She snaps in frustration, "You do this all the time. You never understand. This always happens!" Just like that, the frustration intensifies and an argument starts. If he had known that all she needed was for him to listen attentively and care about her distress, the argument would not have happened. On the other hand, she could have prevented the battle if she had said,

"I have a problem at work . . . but keep your superhero Problem-Solving-Man costume in the phone booth. It is not that I have a problem that I can't solve. I'm not stupid!

I can solve that problem. However, it is the problem that the problem causes. The problem is that the first problem causes me to feel diminished, to feel that I am not valued. It hurts my sense of self-worth and causes me distress. And since you are my life partner, I need and want you to nurture me so that distress can go away.

So shut up and listen! Sit close to me. Hold my hands and pat them. Gaze deeply into my eyes. Nod your head a lot, and every once in while say, 'um hmmm.' And after a few minutes everything will be okay. Then I will go back to work and solve the problem by myself, because I am not stupid!"

The communication, "I have a problem at work," was the prelude to expressing distress. It may not even be a tantrum, but the healthy expressing of the upset or stress from the problem. The loving Gallant Knight becomes activated by a perceived opportunity to rescue the Damsel-in-Distress and slay her Dragon problem. She rejected his help, because she refused to accept being patronized in that weak and ineffectual role. She was insulted and angry, and he felt punished for trying to help. They hop a ride on the Pain Train of couples' communication failures. What starts out as a call for compassion and empathy was responded to with problem-solving suggestions and turned into simultaneous upset tantrums, also known as a fight.

Experiences formulate the instinctual response of children and adults. Affirmative and empowering intervention create positive instincts in infancy that will replicate action throughout childhood into adulthood.

The needs to be the rescuer or to be rescued are among many potentially problematic instincts that are also developed in childhood. Butler (1995) describes an adult's reflective process to recover from feelings of helplessness that triggered her tantrums:

> When she lost her temper she felt utterly helpless inside, just as she used to feel when her sister lost her temper with her. As a child, this made Sandra feel both frightened and powerless—helpless. The feeling of helplessness was very similar to how she now felt, occasionally when her partner insisted on having his own way regardless of what she wanted. She felt so helpless that she wanted to scream, just as her sister had screamed at her . . . understanding the similarity in feeling between how she had sometimes felt with her sister and . . . now . . . felt with her partner, reassured her and helped her to manage her uncontrollable tempers. Understanding their origin had a profound effect because it enabled her to make use of her adult voice to free herself from the old pattern . . . 'I know where this comes from'. . . . Her temper tantrums quickly became less dramatic, and less frequent. (p. 152)

Identifying and resisting frightened instincts from a vulnerable childhood empowered Sandra. She distanced herself from her old helpless role. Sandra developed her own one-minute temper tantrum solution for her adult tantrums through knowledge of her power and control in the present.

CHAPTER HIGHLIGHTS

- Helpless tantrums are an expression of the pervasive underlying despair and fear that a child may feel.

- Validating distress when the underlying issue is despair serves to validate helplessness, which increases the despair.

- Helpless individuals develop an anxious vulnerability, which draws further bullying and exploitation.

- Rescuing children confirms the helplessness of the children and takes away opportunities to learn how to handle conflict.

- When children throw helpless tantrums, empowerment guides them to gain competency and the resultant self-esteem in handling threats.

Stress and the Catchartic Tantrum

11

Releasing the Cathartic Tantrums

Remember my lunchbox. Forgot it last week. Mom was mad.

"Bye, Jani."

Put the spelling book in my backpack. Another test tomorrow . . . (sigh). And the homework sheet. There's Nate. Waving at me. Robi's my name, but don't wear it out. Yeah, yeah . . . I guess I have to say something to him . . .

"Bye, Nate."

Stupid Nate the Gnat bugging me at recess. Now you're smiling. . . . Remember my homework. Dad's going to pick us up late . . . at 3:15? At 3:20? I think?

"See you tomorrow, Razi."

OK. Don't forget the cleats for soccer practice. At the other field, not the regular one.

"Yes, Miss Tagore, I'll return the book to the library."

Meet sister at the day care. Make sure she has her jacket. Hope she's ready.

"Yeah, Sumi, I'll bring it tomorrow."

Ask Mom or Dad to sign the permission slip. Can't go without it. Last chance tomorrow. Bring a change of clothes for getting wet. Bring money. Do I have any? Come to school 15 minutes early for the field trip . . . field trip tomorrow? Or is it Wednesday? Hmmm? Tomorrow? Wednesday?

"What!? Leave me alone . . . Jeez!"

What was that? That's a tantrum, but it's a tantrum unlike the other tantrums. Robi is just "boiling over—there are some days when you just know your child is heading for a tantrum. It can almost feel like they're determined to have one. Your child may be emotionally overloaded by her angry feelings and a tantrum seems inevitable as a result" (BBC, 2007). Overload happens. For children's emotional and psychological health, you need to allow overload, while risking them boiling over occasionally. You need to stress them, disappoint them, allow them to be frustrated, and make sure that they experience failure! Stress does not destroy people; constant unremitting stress is destructive. Stress and disappointment are a part of life, and the ability to tolerate and deal with stress defines success in life. Protecting children from stress eliminates the opportunity and challenge of learning how to deal with it. Things get difficult or complicated and a child declares, "That's not fair!" Life is supposed to be fair? Adults have to protect children from unfairness? Recognizing unfairness means accepting the limitations of life. Dealing with disappointments challenges children to move forward to seize the power and control in life that they can have.

> Protecting children from stress eliminates the opportunity and challenge of learning how to deal with it.

Frustration is also no fun. However, when people go through frustration and are able to persevere and succeed in a task, they gain much self-esteem. Constant frustration is unhealthy, but is also an important part of growth. A 100 percent success is not possible. Children need to be comfortable enough with and experience failure and discover that they can still survive failing.

When children fail, persevere, and eventually succeed, they acquire the most powerful lessons about their abilities and competence. Kwa-li frowns and struggles to get the puzzle together. It was so hard not to intervene to help. "No! Self!" the toddler insists. She wants to do by herself. Finally it all fit together! What a look of delight and triumph! She responded to stress, disappointment, frustration, and failure with continued effort that led to success.

How well do you handle stress? Challenge? A director told me about a scary situation that happened at her preschool. They received a report that there was someone in the neighborhood with a gun. Their playground was adjacent to the street, separated only by a cyclone fence. Five teachers quickly began gathering the children to bring them inside. The sixth teacher panicked and ran inside without helping with the children. She abandoned the children! The director initially defended her, saying, "She is usually a very good teacher. She is usually quite reliable and creative." So she was great when there was no crisis or stress. So what!? However, when she was needed most, under stress in crisis, she failed her most fundamental role of protecting children. Most adults are good parents or good teachers when they are not under stress. Unfortunately, being a caregiver, guide, or mentor to children is largely about being under stress! When children are stressed, adults become stressed. When adults are stressed, children become stressed. Children often haven't learned how to handle stress well, so it is up to the adult to prevent a negative cycle of poor stress responses from developing.

> Children often haven't learned how to handle stress well, so it is up to the adult to prevent a negative cycle of poor stress responses from developing.

STRESS RESPONSE STYLES

The issue is not if there is stress but what to do with inevitable stress. Individuals develop habitual stress response styles. Is your or the child's response style effective and functional? Or is it ineffective, dysfunctional, and possibly harmful? Certain stress responses tend to build or increase stress rather than release or relieve it. Stress builders include the following:

1. Denial. Pretending that one is not stressed or accumulating stress, or denying a situation or experience as stressful.

2. Intensification. Intensifying behavior or the response to stress, even though it has been ineffective.

3. Avoidance behavior. Avoiding confronting, dealing with, or addressing the stress or problem.

4. Hypervigilance. By being extra vigilant, one hopes to see and avoid potential stresses or problems before they happen.

5. Passive-aggressive action. Instead of overtly fighting back or addressing the problem or the other person(s), an individual does

things such as moving slowly or gossiping to aggravate or frustrate the other person.

6. Codependent behavior. An individual tries to gain emotional obligation from other people by being extremely generous and attentive. The hope is that the other person will reciprocate the treatment.

With problematic stress-building habits, release may be in an inappropriate manner. A cathartic temper tantrum is likely. On the other hand, if the individual has solid stress-releasing habits, excessive stress is less likely to accrue and is more likely to express in less self-destructive or socially intrusive ways. Positive stress releasing responses include the following:

STRESS-RELEASING RESPONSES

1. Proactive action. Any action or behavior that increases power and control tends to reduce stress.

2. Physical release. Physical activity releases chemicals, such as endorphins, in the body that affect positive mood.

3. Cathartic release. Accumulated emotional energy, psychological, or cognitive energy in addition to physical energy or stress is released regularly rather than held.

4. Breathing. Deep breathing decreases and release muscle tension. The Lamaze method teaches deep breathing to reduce pain during childbirth.

5. Rest. Sometimes, people just don't rest enough. Hard work creates a stressed body, mind, and spirit, not to mention relationships. As these break down, fatigue sets in. The fatigue affects mood and performance problems, creating additional issues and stress.

6. Self-nurturing. Self-nurturing consists of functional behaviors to calm or confirm: specific activities, acquisition of things, sensory experiences (including dark chocolate, a hot bath, good music), and fulfillment of interpersonal connections. Or the self-nurturing may also include symbolic behaviors that build or reconfirm self-esteem.

7. Seeking help. Stress accumulates when challenges are beyond one's capacity. Getting help may be necessary. One's self-definition or identification as self-sufficient precludes some individuals from asking for help. Other people may be unaware of their stress or not know how to ask for help.

8. Understanding or insight. Stress builds when individuals don't understand why things are happening or why they are being treated in a certain way. People are more likely to accept the challenges of life and relationships with understanding, recognizing what they can and cannot change.

Some children are more sensitive to stimulation that creates stress because of a temperamental trait such as low-sensory threshold or another issue. Children with Asperger syndrome are

> often hypersensitive to sound or visual stimuli, such as fluorescent lights, and may respond negatively when overloaded with these types of sensory stimuli. Parents and teachers have reported behavior problems associated with these children's fear of anticipated unpleasant sensory stimuli such as city whistle signals, chimes, or fire alarms that are sounded at certain times . . . have a strong and obsessive preference for certain foods and textures (e.g., child will only wear clothes made of certain fabrics or cannot tolerate clothing tags touching the skin) . . . (Myles & Southwick, 2005, p. 16)

Regardless of how stress accumulates, the person needs to accept using stress-releasing mechanisms and behaviors. Only with recognition that one is under stress or accumulating stress can one begin to release stress in a healthy way. Some individuals, especially children, may be instinctively releasing stress with their behaviors, which include tantrums. Children often need guidance how to release stress appropriately and to avoid accumulating too much stress. Although eliminating stress altogether is impossible, people can learn how to respond well to stress.

THE CATHARTIC TANTRUM

Are you okay?
  Just give me a minute.

What's wrong? Has something happened?
  I just need a little time for myself.

Is there something I can do? Do you need to talk?
  No, I'll be okay in a little bit.

Are you sure?
  Yes, I'll be okay.

You look a little upset. You need a little help? It'll be okay.
     I know I'll be okay. I told you that.

Is something bothering you?
     *Yes, something is bothering me. YOU are bothering me! If you just
leave me alone for a little bit and I'll finish being bothered . . . upset . . .
not okay . . . by myself! If you stop getting in the way of me doing what
I need to do, I will do what I need to do . . . and I will be okay. If you will
finally get out of the way, so I can do it. IN A MINUTE!*

Some people accumulate stress readily, whereas others release stress readily. There may be family or other group cultural rules about expressing or
handling stress. Some individuals, especially teachers, believe they are
obligated to hold tremendous amounts of stress. Some teachers and parents seem to think that they are supposed to be martyrs. Do you know
what happens to martyrs? They get to
die! But first, they get to suffer a lot! On
the other hand, consider the status!
A lack of appreciation or acknowledgment, added to the overload of stress,
can lead to resentment that prompts caregiver temper tantrums. This is
the consequence of not recognizing when one is accumulating stress, not
taking permission to release stress, and perhaps also not knowing how to
release it appropriately.

> There may be family or other group cultural
> rules about expressing or handling stress.

Babies feel without the intellectual ability to know what they are
feeling. Conceptualization of feelings such as happiness, sadness, fear,
and stress are difficult for young children. Basic nurturing processes
include feedback, also known as emotional mirroring. "Oh, you don't
feel very good" is the feedback and labeling the baby gets when upset or
sick. "Aren't you a happy baby!" helps the baby understand what the
serotonin surge in his or her brain is doing. "So mad you can't reach
it," you tell the baby screaming trying to get the rattle. This feedback
evolves as a child gets older, helping develop increased self-awareness
for social-emotional development. Simultaneously, a child needs to be
guided to develop healthy methods for releasing accumulated stress.
Temper tantrums, overeating, aggressive social behavior, and substance
abuse are to be avoided as inappropriate, self-destructive, and socially
disruptive mechanisms to release stress. Hit the books, the track,
the tennis ball, or the punching bag. Don't hit your sister, the bottle, or
the casino.

If a person is throwing a cathartic temper tantrum, he or she is
already releasing stress. Intuitive permission releases the tantrum or the

pent-up energy. Discipline becomes necessary if the expression, acting out, or
tantrum is inappropriate. If inappropriate, then intervention is to guide the person's behavior toward individually and
socially healthy choices.

> If a person is throwing a cathartic temper
> tantrum, he or she is already releasing
> stress. Intuitive permission releases the
> tantrum or the pent-up energy.

Are you okay?
 Just give me a minute.

What's wrong? Has something happened?
 I just need a little time for myself.

Okay. Let me know if you need anything. I'll check back with you in a
couple of minutes. Is that enough time?
 Sure, I'll be okay in a couple of minutes.

Or . . .

Okay. But you're making too much noise for the other kids to study.
You can go over there, take care of yourself. Come back when you're
ready. I'll check in with you in a little bit.
 Okay.

Or . . .

Okay. You can have a couple of minutes of quiet time. And you need to
get back to your work or you won't be able to finish and get your free
time. I know you want your free time, so don't take too long.

In the first response, the helpful person is attentive, caring, and available, and then essentially gets out of the way so the individual can release
stress without interference. In the second response, the helpful person is
still attentive, caring, and available, but also recognizes that the tantrum
(crying, for example) will be distracting and disruptive to the other children. The child is guided to express feelings while not disrupting the classroom. In the third response, the helpful person is still attentive, caring,
and available, and guides the tantruming person so that he or she won't
suffer a new negative consequence of not finishing work and missing free
time. Guidance to limit the tantrum's length, but not to stop the tantrum
altogether, honors the need for stress release and precludes additional
negative consequences. Another one-minute temper tantrum solution!

CHAPTER HIGHLIGHTS

- Children need to experience stress, frustration, failure, and disappointment to grow strength and self-esteem.

- There are response styles that increase stress, and there are response styles that decrease stress.

- Cathartic tantrums occur with release when an individual becomes overloaded with stress.

- While a person is having a cathartic temper tantrum, he or she may be already taking care of himself or herself by releasing the stress.

- Children having a cathartic tantrum may need guidance as to how to release the stress appropriately.

Getting It Wrong **12** and Getting It Right

GETTING IT WRONG!

"No, no, no, no! Ahhhhhhh! Henry took my toy! I was playing with it. He didn't ask. Stop it! Make him give it back! Ahhhhhhh! AHHHHHHHH!" (Another wonderful day in the classroom neighborhood—not!)

If you know what kind of temper tantrum is going on, then you use the underlying issue to efficiently implement the logical interventions for that tantrum. As you become conceptually clear and experienced, you should be able to recognize the tantrum type within seconds.

1. A manipulative tantrum is best handled by setting limits for getting appropriate versus inappropriate power and control.

2. An upset tantrum is best handled by nurturing or validating the individual in distress.

3. A helpless tantrum is best served by empowering the individual against despair to care for himself or herself.

4. A cathartic tantrum is best served by giving permission and guidance how to best release built-up stress.

However, most tantrums are not purely one type or another, but possess elements of some or all four types of tantrums. One can feel distress when out of control and one can feel helpless without power and control. Distress can evolve into despair. Built-up stress can turn into distress as well. However, most tantrums have a primary underlying issue, which, when addressed, will subside with simultaneous learning of appropriate social-emotional skills. Correct diagnosis leads to resolution, whereas

> Most tantrums are not purely one type or another but possess elements of some or all four types of tantrums.

> Most tantrums have a primary underlying issue, which, when addressed, will subside with simultaneous learning of appropriate social-emotional skills.

misdiagnosis often causes greater problems, including inefficiency and ineffective intervention. Very much, not a one-minute solution in such cases! Some individuals attempt to resolve this diagnostic challenge by trying out the intervention suggested by their tentative guess. Since this approach may be necessary, the following describes what happens when the response matches and mismatches the type of temper tantrum:

1. Setting Boundaries

- Is effective for a **manipulative tantrum** to stop inappropriate attempts **to gain power and control.**

However, setting boundaries creates problems for other types of tantrums.

- If it is actually an **upset tantrum**, then setting boundaries may intensify distress and even create despair. Adults who feel threatened when not in control are more likely to misdiagnose any tantrum as a manipulative tantrum. Many people, including teachers, parents, administrators, and supervisors, who use a hard-line approach not only set boundaries but also threaten and punish. The distressed person needing nurturing instead experiences dismissal from harsh, insensitive boundaries. Nurturing can coincide with setting boundaries. The emphasis with an upset tantrum, however, should be on nurturing the person.
- If it is actually a **helpless tantrum**, then boundaries set do not address the underlying despair. The limits define what can or cannot be done when agitated but not address the sense of impotence in life. The individual may get power and control in the immediate situation (get the ball or an additional snack), but the underlying and pervasive sense of being helpless persists. The individual experiences boundaries as further proof of being helpless in the world, and despair deepens.
- If it is actually a **cathartic tantrum**, then boundaries are set although none may be necessary. You might set firm or harsh limits, when more general guidelines would be sufficient to release stress in some manner not self-destructive or harmful to others.

Harsh limits are distracting and actually interfere with the stress release of a cathartic tantrum.

2. Nurturing or Validating

- Is effective for an **upset tantrum** as it soothes the **underlying distress**.

However, nurturing or validating creates problems for other types of tantrums.

- If it is actually a **manipulative tantrum**, the power- and control-seeking individual may use the caring individual to manipulate the nurturer, a particularly odious reaction. Many individuals seek to love the other person into a more stable and happier place. The manipulative individual threatens others with "I don't like you any-more." Emotional blackmail and the bait and switch of affection corrupt relationships. The manipulative person learns that feigned upset is effective for gaining power and control. Care and nurturing creates problems only when adults acquiesce to unreasonable demands.
- If it is actually a **helpless tantrum**, nurturing and validating behavior, rather than a soothing individual, confirms his or her essential helplessness. This creates the greatest potential for damage. With helpless tantrums, all inappropriate responses cause intensified despair. Compassion is important, but only with the challenge of empowerment.
- If it is actually a **cathartic tantrum**, then attempts to nurture can be distracting and interfere with the stress-release process. Your concern is reassuring but not essential. In a cathartic tantrum, the individual acts out to release stress, not to demand a response. Back off if there is indication that the stress-release process will complete without help. Otherwise, nurturing becomes intrusive and the person may shift from a cathartic tantrum to being annoyed at you!

3. Empowering by Offering
Options or Requiring Proactive Behavior

- Is effective for a **helpless tantrum**, because it **counters feelings of desperation**.

However, empowering by offering options or requiring proactive behavior creates problems for other types of tantrums.

- If it actually is a **manipulative tantrum**, then offers of options, philosophical rules, and values for empowerment will be dismissed. With a manipulative tantrum, power and control demands are immediate, whereas long-term issues are irrelevant. The manipulative tantrumer is motivated only in getting his or her way in the moment—in getting power, not empowerment. Unable to delay gratification, he or she may intensify anger and/or use adult offerings to continue manipulations.

- If it actually is an **upset tantrum**, then suggestions for empowerment will cause greater frustration. The distressed child is not seeking mastery—that is, a sense of potency in the world and life. Despite good intentions, suggestions further invalidate the person in distress. Often the upset person is unable to articulate and direct the potential helper to the emotional distress. A caring adult may intercede to solve a problem, only to find that the child stays distressed. If the adult insists that the child should be fine because the problem seems to have been solved, the distress will intensify. Saying "You got what you wanted. Why are you still upset?" will further upset the child.

- If it actually is a **cathartic tantrum**, then empowering can be distracting. Offering help implies that the person is vulnerable or needy. Individuals may feel insulted or become defensive by the inadvertent blow to his or her self-definition, identity, and self-esteem.

4. Giving Permission and Guidance (or Tolerating)

- Is effective for a **cathartic tantrum**, because it helps a child to **release built-up stress**.

However, giving permission and guidance or tolerating creates problems for other types of tantrums.

- If it is actually a **manipulative tantrum**, then the expectation that the person will "get over it" by himself or herself will not be met. Power and control drives, rather than dissipating, may get more extreme. An angry voice morphs into screaming, stomping around, and hitting. Limit and boundary setting, essential to address a manipulative tantrum, is not activated. The tantruming person over time will feel more enraged.

- If it actually is an **upset tantrum**, then any guidance facilitating the release of stress will not address the underlying distress of the upset tantrum. The distress will intensify, possibly leading to despair.

- If it is actually a **helpless tantrum**, then permission and guidance for the despairing individual to release stress will cause the individual to feel not only misunderstood but also abandoned. Despair will exacerbate.

Here is the same information presented in chart form.

<table>
<thead>
<tr>
<th>Effectiveness or Resultant Problem to Adult</th>
<th></th>
<th>Manipulative Tantrum</th>
<th>Upset Tantrum</th>
<th>Helpless Tantrum</th>
<th>Cathartic Tantrum</th>
</tr>
</thead>
<tbody>
<tr>
<td rowspan="4">Response or Intervention</td>
<td>1. Set Boundaries</td>
<td>**EFFECTIVE**</td>
<td>Problem: Child intensifies distress and potentially degenerates into despair</td>
<td>Problem: Child feels helplessness confirmed and deepening despair</td>
<td>Problem: Child distracted from his or her stress-release behaviors because of adult intervention</td>
</tr>
<tr>
<td>2. Nurture or Validate</td>
<td>Problem: Child uses adult nurturing to further manipulate</td>
<td>**EFFECTIVE**</td>
<td>Problem: Child experiences validation of despair, leading to further deepening of despair</td>
<td>Problem: Child experiences minor distraction or annoyance</td>
</tr>
<tr>
<td>3. Empower</td>
<td>Problem: Child intensifies anger and continues attempts to manipulate</td>
<td>Problem: Child has greater distress and frustration</td>
<td>**EFFECTIVE**</td>
<td>Problem: Child distracted from stress-release behaviors and potentially insulted</td>
</tr>
<tr>
<td>4. Give Permission and Guidance</td>
<td>Problem: Child increases anger and attempts to manipulate</td>
<td>Problem: Child's distress increases, and there is potential of distress turning into despair</td>
<td>Problem: Child feels abandoned and despair increases</td>
<td>**EFFECTIVE**</td>
</tr>
</tbody>
</table>

CHILD RESPONSES TO MISGUIDED INTERVENTIONS

Misdiagnosing a manipulative tantrum: In general, if adults misdiagnose a manipulative tantrum as any other tantrum, the individual will persist in using whatever advantage or openings gained from misguided and ineffective responses. Repeated manipulations, threats, and demands, despite adult interventions, reveal the true nature of the power-seeking tantrum and allow adults to recover from the misdiagnosis. After boundaries are established, consequences may have to follow before the tantruming and power-seeking behavior terminates.

> If adults misdiagnose a manipulative tantrum as any other tantrum, the individual will persist in using whatever advantage or openings gained from misguided and ineffective responses.

Misdiagnosing an upset tantrum: If an upset tantrum is misdiagnosed as one of the other three tantrums, children's distress needs will not be met by caring and reparative adult nurturing. Distress will continue, and children will continue to express the need for nurturing to adults. Children's most fundamental emotional and psychological need is to know that they and especially their distress matter to their caregivers and they expect that these adults will strive mightily to meet their needs and soothe their distress. Thus, misdiagnosing an upset temper tantrum potentially causes great emotional damage to individuals and significant problems in the discipline or community situation. Unmet distress needs can also intensify and transform into despair.

> Children's most fundamental emotional and psychological need is to know that they and especially their distress matter to their caregivers.

Misdiagnosing a helpless tantrum: If a child's desperation increases in response to an intervention, then adults have failed to recognize that it was a helpless tantrum. The practice and experience of competency is the only way a person learns that he or she is capable and powerful in his or her world. A child's helpless tantrum of despair is not satisfied when the child gets his or her way, whereas a manipulative tantrum would be satisfied. Nurturing soothes the distress-based upset tantrum, but often only intensifies the agitated and disruptive energy of despair. The stress of despair does not run its own course, whereas the stress of a cathartic tantrum can.

Misdiagnosing a cathartic tantrum: If adults misdiagnose a cathartic tantrum and subsequently intervene as if it were one of the other tantrums, they ordinarily get some feedback that the individual just needs to release the energy . . . if only others would get out of the way! A cathartic tantrum lacks a compelling intense energy present in the three other temper tantrum types. The underlying need is to release built-up energy or stress rather than the manifestation of distress, despair, or power and control needs.

GETTING IT RIGHT WHEN NOT SURE

Least restrictive environment is the requirement established in court rulings of federal law that children with disabilities receive their education in regular classes (U.S. Code, Title 20). A mainstream class is assumed to be the most appropriate situation for a child unless it is proven inadequate to meet the child's needs. *Primum non nocere* in Latin is derived from an interpretation of the Hippocratic Oath written by Hippocrates, the father of medicine, in the fourth century BC, or by one of his students, which translates as "First, do no harm" (Records, 2007). If you cannot tell which type of temper tantrum is occurring, assume the simplest underlying issue and respond first with the intervention that would cause the least harm if incorrect. Certain incorrect misdiagnoses cause greater problems for everyone rather than resolving tantrums. When you are not sure, follow this sequence to figure this out and resolve the tantrum:

> If you cannot tell which type of temper tantrum is occurring, assume the simplest underlying issue and respond first with the intervention that would cause the least harm if incorrect.

First, assume it is an upset tantrum (Plan A) and validate and nurture the child's apparent distress. If correct, the validation and nurturing will soothe the distress and the child will stop tantruming. He or she may become sad, but sadness is a more stable emotion that doesn't express in tantrums, whereas distress does. The assumption of an upset tantrum leads to relatively harmless interventions even if found ineffective. On the other hand, missing distress is extremely harmful, tending to amplify feelings of abandonment and rejection. Ongoing adult neglect can deepen distress into a fundamental despair and pervasive worthlessness throughout and beyond childhood.

> If the response reveals that the assumption of an upset tantrum was incorrect, then *the child's behavior will also reveal which of the other three types of tantrum is occurring.*

Second, if the response reveals that the assumption of an upset tantrum was incorrect, then *the child's behavior will also reveal which of the other three types of tantrum is occurring.* If the child does not respond to being nurtured and validated by calming down, observe the response. If the child

- pauses to see if the adult is complying or acquiescing,
- intensifies the volume or physicality of the tantrum or more overtly disrupts the environment,
- and/or otherwise shows further or new manipulative behavior,

then it is probably a **manipulative tantrum** with the primary underlying issue of the child seeking power and control inappropriately. Consequently, the intervention is to set limits and boundaries for the child (Plan B).

On the other hand, if the child

- continues with similar or even more intensified behavior despite nurturing,
- uses a whining tone,
- sounds defeated,
- expresses hopelessness, a sense of repeated experiences of injustice and unfairness,
- asserts the systematic lack of attention or acknowledgment of his or her needs,
- names other individuals as the favored and undeserving benefactors of arbitrary decisions,
- and/or uses the following descriptive terminology: "always," "never," or "all the time,"

then it is probably a **helpless tantrum** with the primary underlying issue of despair. Consequently, the intervention is to empower the child (Plan C). "This is what you need to do. You chose to do that before, which is why this is happening now. If you want it to happen differently, this is what you need to do. If you choose not to do that, then later you will continue to not get what you want."

Another set of responses would indicate the fourth different type of temper tantrum. If the child

- seems somewhat surprised at the adult intervention and seeks to continue the behavior without any demands,
- expresses appreciation, annoyance, or indifference to the nurturing,
- and/or asserts the need for and the confidence in his or her process,

then it is probably a **cathartic tantrum** with the primary underlying issue being that the child is loaded up with stress and is releasing it.

Consequently, the intervention is to give permission to the child if he or she is failing to release stress and/or give the child guidance how to release the stress appropriately (Plan D). This can be a very quick process.

THE ONE-MINUTE TEMPER TANTRUM SOLUTION

"No, no, no, no! Ahhhhhhh! Henry took my toy! I was playing with it. He didn't ask. Stop it! Make him give it back! Ahhhhhhh! AHHHHHHHH!" (Another wonderful day in the classroom neighborhood—not!)

When in doubt, assume that it is an upset tantrum, Plan A.

"I hear you Dennis. I know you want the ball. It's not nice to have it taken away from you like that. That makes you sad. Okay, let's see what we can do about it."

Child Reaction A: Dennis calms down because he experiences you acknowledging his distress and can feel the nurturing energy. He's sad still but is more settled as he awaits what you will do. It is much easier to handle a situation or conflict when Dennis is not going crazy. Nailed it! Nurturing and validation did the trick because of the correct diagnosis of this as an upset temper tantrum.

However if the diagnosis had been incorrect, Dennis would give cues to what was actually going on within him. Depending on how he reacts to your response, you can determine what type of tantrum was happening. The following repeats the original adult response (Plan A) three times and describes in turn the three different child reactions that show that it was an inappropriate intervention. Then it describes how to implement Plan B, Plan C, or Plan D, as is appropriate.

"I hear you, Dennis. I know you want the ball. It's not nice to have it taken away from you like that. Getting it taken away like that makes you sad. Okay, let's see what we can do about it."

Child Reaction B: Instead of calming down, Dennis says, "I want that toy. Ahhhhhh! Give me that toy. Make him give it back to me! I want it now! NOW! AHHHHH!" Dennis grabs at the toy and takes a swing at the other kid. Well, that didn't work! Dennis is intensifying his yelling and screaming and has stepped up to physical aggression to get the toy. He may have every right to have a grievance against the child, but trying to hit is not acceptable. Not an upset temper tantrum, but Dennis's reaction to your first intervention is clearly about reasserting and intensifying behavior to get power and control inappropriately. It's a manipulative tantrum, so you set clear limits. Plan B—read the riot act!

> *"Dennis, you may not hit Henry. We can work this out about the toy, but you will not get the toy as long as you are screaming. Stop screaming now. If you cannot stop screaming or trying to hit, you will not get the toy. You will not get to play. You have to use your words. You understand? Do you want to work this out or do you want to scream and hit? If you need to scream and hit, then you will have to take a break over there until you're ready to behave differently."*

And if Dennis continues to choose to be unreasonable with his attempts to gain power and control, make sure he does not get power and control. If he chooses to be reasonable, then you will help him. The tantrum becomes a learning opportunity to benefit Dennis now and in his future relationships. On the other hand, you might get another reaction:

> *"I hear you Dennis. I know you want the ball. It's not nice to have it taken away from you like that. Getting it taken away like that makes you sad. Okay, let's see what we can do about it."*

Child Reaction C: Instead of calming down, Dennis whines, "I always get things taken away from me. I never get to play with what I want. Everyone does this all the time to me! It's not fair! Waaaaaaaah!" Life sure is tough on a kid. First, you're short and then you grow up and have to pay taxes! Didn't he know that we're all card-carrying members of the World Conspiracy to Harass Dennis? Henry can be pretty aggressive. He's no innocent. But Dennis can easily become a perpetual victim when adults do too much to rescue him. He needs to find his own power, not get his power and control solely through depending on others to come to the rescue. Plan C—empowers him.

> *Okay, Dennis, I know you want the ball. You need to tell Henry to give it back to you. Tell him to give the ball back right now, because you had it first. Tell him if he cannot give you the ball by himself, you will get help from me. Henry, Dennis wants to talk to you. Okay, Dennis, go talk to Henry and get the ball back.*

You set the stage for Dennis, by prompting Henry that Dennis wants to talk to him, but you do not resolve the conflict for Dennis. Dennis has been empowered with the authority to demand the ball back, and you are available as the backup enforcement if Henry refuses to comply. However, it is mandatory for Dennis to make it happen. If Dennis can do so, he has taken power. If he doesn't, you remind him that he has declined power that was available for him. Only if he has tried to get the ball through appropriate communication, do you, upon his request, facilitate getting the ball from Henry. If Dennis cannot try, then you take the ball away from both Henry and Dennis. Henry doesn't get it either, because he was inappropriate as well. Point out to both children that no one gets the ball, because no one has behaved appropriately. Remind Dennis again of what he needs to do next time to get the ball. Last, there is one other possible reaction:

> *"I hear you, Dennis. I know you want the ball. It's not nice to have it taken away from you like that. Getting it taken away like that makes you sad. Okay, let's see what we can do about it."*

Child Reaction D: Instead of calming down, Dennis says, "Huh? What? I just wanted the ball. Henry, please may I have the ball back?" Dennis seems to know how to handle it. You don't have to do anything. He was blowing off steam. Or he might have said, "I just get so mad. Sorry I was yelling." Plan D—give him guidance how to express himself when angry.

> *"That's right, Dennis. Yelling is not the way to get the ball back. When you're mad, try taking a couple of deep breaths. Think a little bit before doing anything. Or you can take a little break first."*

Dennis might have said nothing in response but gotten red in the face and starting to squeal a little bit! So you might say,

> *"It's okay to be mad, Dennis. It's okay to say you're mad. You don't have to hold it in. Just tell Henry that you don't like it."*

Dennis says, "I . . . don't . . . like . . . that . . . please . . . give . . . me . . . the . . . ball . . . back." Dennis lets out his stress or is given permission to do so. He has been guided how to do so appropriately. He calms down and gets the ball back, too. A highly efficient and effective temper tantrum resolution—perhaps literally—a one-minute temper tantrum solution even though you didn't know what type of temper tantrum it was in the beginning!

CHAPTER HIGHLIGHTS

- Setting boundaries is effective for a manipulative tantrum but may intensify distress, deepen despair, or be distracting for other tantrum types.

- Nurturing or validating is effective for an upset tantrum but may be used to manipulate, confirm essential helplessness, or distract or interfere for other tantrum types.

- Empowering is effective for helpless tantrums but may intensify anger, continued manipulations, greater frustration, distraction, or insult for other tantrum types.

- Giving permission and guidance is effective for a cathartic tantrum but may create more extreme behavior, intensify distress, or exacerbate despair for other tantrum types.

- When you are not sure what type of tantrum is occurring, assume and respond first that it is an upset tantrum. If nurturing or validating is ineffective, then the behavior of the individual will direct you to a correct determination of the type of tantrum.

Conclusion

This book promotes a broad definition of what a temper tantrum may be about. It can be a classic temper tantrum with a body flung onto the floor, fists flailing, and punctuated with intense screams. But it can also be the silent treatment, passive-aggressive behavior, over- or undereating, self-mutilation, substance abuse, and more. Temper tantrums are part of a larger spectrum of behaviors and reactions. Any temper tantrum is an expression of and an attempt to meet a need by an individual. Do we care about children's needs or care only about compliant behavior? Greater appreciation of child development principles and compassion for the emotional, psychological, and social damages caused by strictly behavior management philosophies lead to qualitative changes for discipline that are essential to a healthier society. Stopping a temper tantrum does not acknowledge or promote health for the individual, the family, the classroom, and future relationships and communities. Discipline is teaching a disciple how to live a healthy and productive life. As adults, we are the mentors and the children are the disciples. Discipline is not merely about managing an individual's behavior, the household, or classroom dynamics. Brazelton (2005) defines goals as to help children learn to handle tantrums:

> To keep them safe, and to teach them self-control. Children scare themselves with their overwhelming feelings, their loss of control. They humiliate themselves with their limited ways of getting their needs met and of putting up with frustration when they can't have what they want. They are ashamed that they've let important adults down. Protection from such feelings becomes the child's motivation to care about self-control. Later, self-control will be the child's best protection from hurting others. . . . When a young child loses control, he needs our help to believe that he can learn to control himself. He needs our help to keep him from labeling himself as "bad."

Temper tantrums are part of a larger spectrum of behaviors and reactions. Any temper tantrum is an expression of and an attempt to meet a need by an individual.

In many harsher prior times and other societies, labeling a child as "bad" was common and even recommended. The focus was to get children to behave as society prescribed, with minimal if any regard to emotional, psychological, or spiritual harm. In a more democratic society without rigid class and caste restrictions, a child's future is not determined by gender, skin color, ethnicity, or their parents' religious, economic, and political beliefs. Children are allowed to develop, to become their own being as they travel their own journeys, discover their own meaning of life, and find their own destinies—and to do so without infringing on and harming others in their search. What a challenge! A healthier and more whole child requires a more progressive community. The National Association for the Education of Young Children (2007) puts it eloquently:

> Children develop and learn best in the context of a community where they are safe and valued, their physical needs are met, and they feel psychologically secure . . . children's development in all areas is influenced by their ability to establish and maintain a limited number of positive, consistent primary relationships with adults and other children. . . . These primary relationships begin in the family but extend over time to include children's teachers and members of the community; therefore, practices that are developmentally appropriate address children's physical, social, and emotional needs as well as their intellectual development.

As children experiment with life and learn, disruptions and mistakes happen. Temper tantrums happen. Disruptions, mistakes, and temper tantrums must happen for children to become full and complete, whether you like it or not. They become growth opportunities. Ignoring, attacking, and stopping temper tantrum without attention to the underlying issues also ignores, attacks, and stops the human energy of the individual.

One of my favorite experiences teaching about the four types of temper tantrums was when I was teaching a series of parent education workshops for a small school. I had taught about temper tantrums in the second workshop of the series. Before the next workshop, a tall man, one of the fathers dressed in a three-piece suit, came up to me with a huge smile on his face. Eyes twinkling with amusement, he told me he was an attorney at a prestigious law firm. He had really enjoyed the workshop on the four different types of tantrums. For the past month, he had watched people throw tantrums at his law firm!

Attorneys, paralegals, bookkeepers, senior partners, and clients all had thrown tantrums. He said he had amazing fun, easily and quickly diagnosing which type of tantrum each had thrown. Best of all, if the tantrum was directed at or involved him, he could quickly figure out not only what type of tantrum it was but efficiently instigate a one-minute temper tantrums solution! It was the most enjoyable month he had ever had at his highly stressful job with highly demanding senior partners and clients with their massive egos and narcissistic energy. And he laughed, "They make dealing with my son's little temper tantrums seem so easy!" He was obviously a great dad who was going to help his son handle his disruptions successfully in the moment and for his future.

And now, I'm going to let you in on a little secret. I had mentioned earlier that all temper tantrums have components of all four types of tantrums in them—with one underlying issue more prominent in any given tantrum—and that a matching intervention should be initiated to handle it. Well, I lied. Setting limits, nurturing or validating, empowering, and giving permission and guidance are not really four different interventions. All the interventions are actually one and the same in that they are nurturing and empowering. Learning appropriate boundaries to gain power and control is empowering. Releasing stress is nurturing. All the interventions nurture a more emotionally, psychologically, and socially competent child who can be a healthier and more productive individual in his or her current and future communities. My old *World Book Encyclopedia Dictionary* (Barnhart, 1963) has two definitions for *nurture:* "to rear; bring up; and care for; foster; train" and "to nourish; feed." All these definitions fit healthy adult responses and discipline for children. A cry, acting out, or a tantrum becomes a cry for help from you to rear, train, and nourish. Respond well to that cry. The children need you. They will challenge you, but they really need you, especially the ones who lose it and tantrum. Responding to teaching or parenting challenges and frustration can cause you to feel a lack of power and control, distress, despair, or an overload of stress. Will you tantrum? Act out a bit? Or will you have some other very human reaction in the spectrum of responses to life's challenges? Dealing with your and their temper tantrums is challenging and may sound more important than dealing with a minor bit of acting out. You need to recognize and accept that tantrums and other behaviors are greater and lesser expressions in the same spectrum. If you can, then you will be greatly empowered to meet the challenge of your very human children; your very human family, friends, and colleagues; and your very human self to be as successful as possible. Watch for those tantrums! All four kinds! But now you've been empowered how to handle them. One more thing . . . the strategies from this book may not get you to a complete solution. However, the more you understand children's motivations and behaviors, the better you can be the teacher or parent they need to guide them. And you may be amazed at how efficiently and effectively you can help children resolve their needs. So maybe it'll take more than one minute. Maybe it'll take . . . two minutes! But what do you care and what does the child care, if it takes a bit more time than hoped, as long as it works? Take one minute to think about that! Good luck!

> Setting limits, nurturing or validating, empowering, and giving permission and guidance are not really four different interventions.

CHAPTER HIGHLIGHTS

- A broad definition of temper tantrums to include a large spectrum of behaviors and reactions promotes better meeting of children's many needs.

- A temper tantrum, acting out, and many other behaviors are individuals' expressions of some need and an attempt to meet that need.

- Discipline serves to get children to behave as society prescribed, including eliminating tantrums, but discipline also needs to promote emotional, psychological, or spiritual health.

- Temper tantrums are growth opportunities for children.

- All responses or interventions for any of the four temper tantrum types are nurturing and empowering.

References

Albrecht, K. M., & Miller, L. G. (2001). *Innovations: The comprehensive infant curriculum: A complete, interactive curriculum for infants from birth to 18 months.* Beltsville, MD: Gryphon House.

American Psychiatric Association. (1994). *Diagnostic and statistical manual of mental disorders* (4th ed.). Washington, DC: Author.

Ashley, S. (2005). *The ADD & ADHD answer book.* Naperville, IL: Sourcebooks.

Audiblox. (2007). *Learning disabilities and difficulties: The emotional scars.* Retrieved October 1, 2007, from http://www.audiblox.com/learning_disabilities.htm

Barnhart, C. L. (Ed.). (1963). *The world book encyclopedia dictionary.* New York: Doubleday.

BBC. (2007). *Tantrum triggers.* Retrieved October 7, 2007, from http://www.bbc.co.uk/parenting/your_kids/toddlers_tantrums.shtml

Brazelton, T. B. (2005). *Teach child how to handle tantrums* [Special feature]. *New York Times.* Retrieved October 1, 2007, from http://findarticles.com/p/articles/mi_qn4188/is_20050523/ai_n14638777

Brazelton, T. B., & Sparrow, J. D. (2005). *Mastering anger and aggression: The Brazelton way.* Cambridge, MA: Da Capo Press.

Bright Horizons Family Solutions. (2007). *Taming temper tantrums.* Retrieved October 18, 2007, from the *e-family news* Web site: http://www.brighthorizons.com/efamily/article.aspx?id=125

Burton, T. (producer). (2005). *Charlie and the chocolate factory* [Motion picture]. United States: Warner Bros.

Butler, G. (1995). *Manage your mind: The mental fitness guide.* Oxford, UK: Oxford University Press.

Carlino, L. J. (director). (1979). *The Great Santini* [Motion picture]. United States: Orion Pictures and Warner Bros.

Carroll, R. T. (2006). *The skeptic's dictionary: Occam's razor.* Retrieved September 19, 2007, from http://skepdic.com/occam.html

Cheng, K., & Myers, K. M. (2005). *Child and adolescent psychiatry: The essentials.* Philadelphia: Lippincott Williams.

Chess, S., & Thomas, A. (1996). *Temperament, theory, and practice.* Philadelphia: Psychology Press.

Clark, C. C. (2007). *Temper tantrums.* Retrieved September 28, 2007, from BellaOnline Web site: http://www.bellaonline.com/articles/art 25312.asp

Coffey, C. E., & Brumback, R. A. (1998). *Textbook of pediatric neuropsychiatry.* Washington, DC: American Psychiatric Association.

Conroy, P. (1976). *The Great Santini.* Boston: Houghton Mifflin.

Cort, R. W. (producer). (1987). *Three men and a baby* [Motion picture]. United States: Touchstone Pictures.

Cosby, B. (host). (1998–2000). *Kids say the darndest things* [Television series]. New York: CBS.

Dr. Seuss. (1957). *The cat in the hat.* New York: Random House.

Dahl, R. (1964). *Charlie and the chocolate factory.* New York: Alfred A. Knopf.

DuPree, J., & Wells, L. (2007). *Understanding temper tantrums.* Retrieved August 2, 2007, from http://www.minti.com/parenting-advice/6937/

Editorial Projects in Education. (2004). *Parent involvement.* Retrieved September 19, 2007, from http://www.edweek.org/rc/issues/parent-involvement/?print=1

Godin, S. (2005). *The big moo.* New York: Penguin.

Grady, B. (2007). *Emotional development and tantrums.* Retrieved September 22, 2007, from http://www.parenting-plus.com/newsletters.htm

Granger, R. H. (1995). *Your child from one to six.* Washington, DC: U.S. Department of Health Education, and Welfare, Office of Human Development Services, Administration for Children, Youth and Families.

Greene, A. (1996, May 21). *Temper tantrums.* Retrieved October 1, 2007, from http://www.drgreene.org/body.cfm?id=21&action=detail&ref=565

Greene, R. W. (2005). *The explosive child: Understanding and helping easily frustrated "chronically inflexible" children.* New York: Harper.

Harrington, R. G. (2004). *Temper tantrums: Guidelines for parents, helping children at home and school II: Handouts for families and educators.* Bethesda, MD: National Association of School Psychologists.

Hart, B. J. (1992). State codes on domestic violence: Analysis, commentary and recommendations. *Juvenile and Family Court Journal, 43*(4), 33.

Herbert, M. (2003). *Typical and atypical development: From conception to adolescence.* Cambridge, MA: Blackwell.

Hoecker, J. L. (2006). *Managing temper tantrums: Advice from a Mayo Clinic specialist.* Retrieved September 26, 2007, from the Mayo Foundation for Medical Education and Research Web site: http://www.mayoclinic.com/health/tantrum/HQ01622

Jackson, S. A. (1993). *Educating young children prenatally exposed to drugs and at risk.* Washington, DC: U.S. Department of Education, Office of Educational Research and Improvement.

Kropp, P. (2001). *I'll be the parent, you be the child: Encourage excellence, set limits, and lighten up.* New York: Perseus.

Lawrence, J. (2007). *Taming temper tantrums.* Retrieved August 21, 2007, from http://www.angelfire.com/ky/touristinfo/tempertantrum.html

Leung, A. K. C., & Fagan, J. E. (1991, August). Temper tantrums. *American Family Physician.* Retrieved October 1, 2007, from http://findarticles.com/p/articles/mi_m3225/is_n2_v44/ai_11197514

Mah, R. (2007). *Difficult behavior in early childhood: Positive discipline for PreK–3 classrooms and beyond.* Thousand Oaks, CA: Corwin Press.

MamasHealth.com. (2007). *What triggers a temper tantrum?* Retrieved September 24, 2007, from http://www.mamashealth.com/child/temper.asp

Marano, H. E. (1995, September/October). Big bad bully. *Psychology Today.* Retrieved October 1, 2007, from http://psychologytoday.com/articles/pto-19950901–000020.html

Motamedi, B. (2007). *A healthy me.* Retrieved June 17, 2007, from www .ahealthyme.com

Myles, B. S., & Southwick, J. (2005). *Asperger's syndrome and difficult moments: Practical solutions for tantrums, rage, and meltdowns.* Shawnee Mission, KS: Autism Aspergers Publishing.

National Association for the Education of Young Children. (2007). *Principles of child development and learning that inform developmentally appropriate practice: Developmentally appropriate practice in early childhood programs serving children from birth through age 8.* Retrieved May 17, 2007, from http://www.naeyc .org/about/positions/dap3.asp

O'Leary, S. G. (1995). Parental discipline mistakes. *Current Directions in Psychological Science, 4*(1), 11–13.

O'Leary, S. G., Slep, A. M. S., & Reid, M. J. (1999). A longitudinal study of mothers' overreactive discipline and toddlers' externalizing behavior. *Journal of Abnormal Child Psychology, 27,* 331–341.

Ollendick, T. H., & Schroeder, C. S. (2003). *Encyclopedia of clinical child and pediatric psychology.* New York: Kluwer Academic/Plenum.

Parrott, L. (2000). *Helping the struggling adolescent: A guide to thirty-six common problems for counselors, pastors, and youth workers.* Grand Rapids, MI: Zondervan.

Pawel, J. J. (2007). *Expert on call.* Retrieved September 24, 2007, from Parent's Toolshop Consulting Web site: http://www.parentstoolshop.com/HTML/tips2.htm

Peurifoy, R. Z. (2005). *Anxiety, phobias, and panic.* New York: Warner Books.

Piaget, J. (1953). *The origin of intelligence in the child.* London: Routledge.

Pollard, I. (2002). *Life, love and children: A practical introduction to bioscience ethics and bioethics.* Norwell, MA: Kluwer Academic.

Potegal, M., & Davidson, R. J. (2003). Temper tantrums in young children: Behavioural composition. *Journal of Developmental and Behavioural Pediatrics, 24,* 140–148.

Raising Children Network. (2006). *Temper tantrums.* Retrieved September 19, 2007, from http://raisingchildren.net.au/articles/temper_tantrums.html

Records, S. (2007). *"First, do no harm": Not in the Hippocratic Oath.* Retrieved October 21, 2007, from http://www.geocities.com/everwild7/noharm.html

Reid, M. J., O'Leary, S. G., & Wolff, L. S. (1994). Effects of maternal distraction and reprimands on toddlers' transgressions and negative affect. *Journal of Abnormal Child Psychology, 22*(2), 237–245.

Ruffin, N. J. (2001). *Human growth and development—A matter of principles* (Publication No. 350–053). Retrieved October 1, 2007, from http://www.ext .vt.edu/pubs/family/350–053/350–053.html

Schmitt, B. D. (2006a). *Temper tantrums.* Retrieved September 1, 2007, from http://www.med.umich.edu/11ibr/pa/pa_btantrum_hhg.htm

Schmitt, B. D. (2006b). *Your child's health.* New York: Bantam Books.

Sears, B. (2006). *Discipline and behavior.* Retrieved September 22, 2007, from http://www.askdrsears.com/html/6/t063300.asp

SmartMomma.com. (2007). *Attention-seeking or demanding tantrum.* Retrieved September 19, 2007, from http://www.smartmomma.com/Toddler/ temper_tantrums.htm

Stevenson, J., & Goodman, R. (2001). Association between behaviour at age 3 years and adult criminality (Developmental Psychopathology Papers, Part 2). *British Journal of Psychiatry, 179,* 197–202.

Stevenson, R. (director). (1964). *Mary Poppins* [Motion picture]. United States: Disney.

Straus, M. A. (1994). *Beating the devil out of them: Corporal punishment in American families in the U.S.* Lexington, MA: Lexington Books.

Straus, M. A., & Stewart, J. H. (1999). Corporal punishment by American parents: National data on prevalence, chronicity, severity, and duration in relation to child and family characteristics. *Clinical Child and Family Psychology Review, 2*(2), 55–70.

Suburban Pediatric Clinic. (2007). *Toddler tips.* Retrieved September 19, 2007, from http://www.suburbanpeds.com/baby_news/2year.pdf.

Thomas, A., Chess, S., & Birch, H. G. (1970). The origin of personality. *Scientific American,* 102–109.

Tiet, Q. Q., Bird, H. R., Hoven, C. W., Moore, R., Wu, P., Wicks, J., et al. (2001). Relationship between specific adverse life events and psychiatric disorders— Statistical data included. *Journal of Abnormal Child Psychology, 29,* 153–164.

Trimble, D. (2001). Making sense in conversations about learning disabilities. *Journal of Marital and Family Therapy, 27*(4), 473–486.

Turecki, S. (1989). *The difficult child.* New York: Bantam Books.

U.S. Code, Title 20 (U.S.C.) Sec. 1412(a)(5)(A), Education, Chapter 33- Education of Individuals with Disabilities, Subchapter II- Assistance for Education of All Children with Disabilities.

U.S. Congress, Office of Technology Assessment. (1986). *Children's mental health: problems and services—A background paper* (OTA-BP-H-33). Washington, DC: Government Printing Office.

Wegmann, J. (2007). *Temper tantrums in children.* Retrieved September 27, 2007, from Discovery Health Web site: http://health.discovery.com/encyclopedias/ illnesses.html?article=2743

Wikler, M. (2003). *How to deal with your spouse's anger.* Retrieved October 1, 2007, from http://www.aish.com/family/marriage/Lion_Taming.asp

Williamson, G. G., Anzalone, M. E., & Hanft, B. E. (2006). *Assessment of sensory processing, praxis, and motor performance* (collaboration report on a framework for early identification and preventive intervention of emotional and developmental challenges). Bethesda: Interdisciplinary Council on Developmental and Learning Disorders.

Woodruff, D., Osher, D., Hoffman, C., Gruner, A., King, M., Snow, S., et al. (1998). *The role of education in a system of care: Effectively serving children with emotional or behavioral disorders* (Systems of Care Promising Practices in Children's Mental Health 1998 Monograph Series). Retrieved August 25, 2007, from http://cecp.air.org/promisingpractices/1998monographs/vol13.pdf

Index

Asperger syndrome, 68, 115
Attachment, 24
Attention deficit disorder (ADD),
    60, 65
Attention deficit hyperactivity
    disorder (ADHD), 40, 46,
    59, 60, 65–67
Attention-seeking tantrum, 31
Autism, 11

Behavioral hierarchy, 12–14
Body language, 94, 95
Boundaries:
    cathartic tantrum, 120–121
    helpless tantrum, 120
    manipulative tantrum, 78,
        88–89, 120
    upset tantrum, 120

Cathartic tantrum:
    boundaries, 120–121
    empowerment, 122
    intervention assessment,
        126–127
    intervention remedies, 78,
        115–117, 119, 122, 123
    misguided interventions, 120–121,
        122, 123, 124–125
    nurturance, 121
    stress-releasing guidance,
        78, 111–118, 119, 122
    stress-releasing responses,
        114–115
    stress response styles, 113–114
    validation, 121
Connection, 94–98
Corporal punishment, 10

Demanding tantrum, 30–31
Despair, 78, 101–109, 119, 121
Developmental factors:
    attachment, 24
    behavioral hierarchy, 12–14
    critical periods, 22–23
    developmental changes, 22, 23
    developmental demands,
        22, 24–25
    developmental energy, 22–27
    developmental principles, 21
    developmental stages, 22–23
    example, 25–26
    intervention assessment, 12–16
    manipulative tantrum, 83–84
    play, 19–21, 25–26
    progressive development,
        22, 23–24
    resiliency, 22, 25–26
    satiation, 22–26
    sequential development, 22–23
    stress effects, 22, 24–25
    tantrum effects, 18–19
    theoretical rules, 21–25
Difficult Behavior in Early Childhood,
    Positive Discipline for PreK–3
    Classrooms and Beyond (Mah),
    5, 73
Difficult Child, The (Turecki), 41
Disruption factors:
    behavioral hierarchy, 12–14
    intervention assessment, 12–16
    tantrum effects, 34–36
Distracter role, 55–56, 57–58
Distraction, 75–77
Distress, 78, 91–99, 119, 121
Dysfunctional system, 53–56

Empowerment:
  cathartic tantrum, 122
  helpless tantrum, 78, 101–103,
    106–109, 121
  manipulative tantrum, 122
  upset tantrum, 122
Environment, 49–52

Facial expression, 94, 95
Family roles, 54–58
Functional system, 52–53

Genetics, 39–40, 41

Helpless tantrum:
  boundaries, 120
  despair, 78, 101–109, 119, 121
  empowerment, 78, 101–103,
    106–109, 121
  helplessness creation, 103–105,
    107–109
  hero role, 107–109
  intervention assessment, 126
  intervention remedies, 78,
    101–103, 105–109,
    119, 121, 123
  misguided interventions, 120, 121,
    123, 124
  nurturance, 121
  self-fulfilling prophecy, 105–107
  stress-releasing guidance, 123
  validation, 121
Hero role:
  helpless tantrum, 107–109
  systemic factors, 54, 57–58

Inattention, 74–75
Indulgence, 72, 101
Instrumental tantrum, 31
Intervention assessment:
  behavioral hierarchy, 12–14
  cathartic tantrum, 126–127
  discipline techniques, 9–10
  factors affecting, 6, 12–16
  helpless tantrum, 126
  manipulative tantrum, 125–126
  misguided interventions, 120–125
  response sequence for, 125–127

tantrum triggers, 11–12
  upset tantrum, 125
Intervention remedies, 71–79
  cathartic tantrum, 78, 115–117,
    119, 122
  distraction, 75–77
  helpless tantrum, 78, 101–103,
    105–109, 119, 121
  inattention, 74–75
  indulgence, 72, 101
  manipulative tantrum, 78, 88–89,
    119, 120
  multi-issue theory, 77–78
  nurturance, 72–73, 101–102
  punishment, 73–74
  shame, 73
  tantrum types, 77–78, 133–134
  upset tantrum, 78, 91–98, 119, 121

K.I.S.S. principle, 14, 32, 35–36

Learning disabilities, 61–65
Lost-child role, 55, 57–58

Mah, R., 5, 73
Manipulative tantrum:
  boundaries, 78, 88–89, 120
  choice consequences, 86–89
  developmental factors, 83–84
  empowerment, 122
  intervention assessment, 125–126
  intervention remedies, 78, 88–89,
    119, 120, 123
  misguided interventions, 121, 122,
    123, 124
  negative behavior, 85–86
  nurturance, 121
  passive-aggressive behavior, 84–86
  power and control, 78, 81–90,
    119, 120
  situational factors, 31, 81–82, 89
  stress-releasing guidance, 122
  validation, 121
Moral factors:
  behavioral hierarchy, 12–14
  intervention assessment, 12–16
  tantrum effects, 67–69
Multi-issue theory, 77–78

Negative behavior, 85–86
Nurturance, 72–73
    cathartic tantrum, 121
    helpless tantrum, 121
    manipulative tantrum, 121
    upset tantrum, 78, 101–102, 121
Nurturer role, 55, 57–58

Occam's razor, 14
One-Minute Temper Tantrum
    Solution, 6–8, 127–129

Passive-aggressive behavior, 84–86
Physical factors:
    behavioral hierarchy, 12–14
    intervention assessment, 12–16
    tantrum effects, 32–33
Physical touch, 94–95
Play, 19–21, 25–26
Power and control, 78, 81–90,
    119, 120
Progressive development,
    22, 23–24
Punishment, 10, 73–74

Rebel role, 56–58
Resiliency, 22, 25–26

Satiation, 22–26
Self-fulfilling prophecy, 105–107
Sequential development, 22–23
Shame, 73
Situational factors:
    behavioral hierarchy, 12–14
    intervention assessment, 12–16
    manipulative tantrum,
        31, 81–82, 89
    tantrum effects, 29–32
Socialization message, 97–98
Specific/specialized factors:
    behavioral hierarchy, 12–14
    child demands, 61
    diagnosis, 59–61, 65–67
    intervention assessment, 12–16
    learning disabilities, 61–65
    misdiagnosis, 63–65
    tantrum effects, 63–67
Stress, 22, 24–25

Stress-releasing guidance:
    cathartic tantrum,
        78, 111–118, 119, 122
    helpless tantrum, 123
    manipulative tantrum, 122
    upset tantrum, 122
Systemic factors:
    behavioral hierarchy, 12–14
    distracter role, 55–56, 57–58
    dysfunctional system, 53–56
    environment, 49–52
    family roles, 54–58
    functional system, 52–53
    hero role, 54, 57–58
    intervention assessment,
        12–16
    lost-child role, 55, 57–58
    nurturer role, 55, 57–58
    parental behavior, 51–52
    rebel role, 56–58
    tantrum effects, 54–56

Temperamental factors:
    behavioral hierarchy, 12–14
    character evaluation, 43
    evaluation traits, 41–42
    family systems, 40–41
    genetics, 39–40, 41
    intervention assessment,
        12–16
    misdiagnosis, 40–41
    tantrum effects, 43–45
    temperamental profiles, 45–47
    temperamental traits, 41–45
    upset tantrum, 92–93
Temper tantrums:
    age of child percentage, 3
    approaches to, 4–6
    average frequency, 3
    average time span, 3
    child support, 3–4
    types, 1–3, 77–78, 131–134
    See also Cathartic tantrum; Helpless
        tantrum; Manipulative
        tantrum; One-Minute Temper
        Tantrum Solution; Upset
        tantrum
Turecki, S., 41

Upset tantrum:
  body language, 94, 95
  boundaries, 120
  connection, 94–98
  distress, 78, 91–99, 119, 121
  empowerment, 122
  facial expression, 94, 95
  intervention assessment, 125
  intervention remedies,
      78, 91–98, 119, 121, 123
  misguided interventions,
      120, 122, 123, 124
  nurturance, 78, 101–102, 121
  physical touch, 94–95

  socialization message, 97–98
  stress-releasing guidance, 122
  temperamental factors, 92–93
  validating message, 94, 96–97
  validation, 78, 91–99, 121
  voice tone, 94, 95–96

Validation:
  cathartic tantrum, 121
  helpless tantrum, 121
  manipulative tantrum, 121
  upset tantrum,
      78, 91–99, 121
Voice tone, 94, 95–96

**CORWIN
PRESS**

The Corwin Press logo—a raven striding across an open book—represents the union of courage and learning. Corwin Press is committed to improving education for all learners by publishing books and other professional development resources for those serving the field of PreK–12 education. By providing practical, hands-on materials, Corwin Press continues to carry out the promise of its motto: **"Helping Educators Do Their Work Better."**